JD's REGENTS PREPARATION, LLC.

-Presents-

INTEGRATED ALGEBRA REVIEW MANUAL

WITH 10 REGENT EXAMS, 8 TOPICALLY ORGANIZED

MAPS TO CORE CURRICULUM CONTENT STRANDS

Cover illustration by James A. Stiehl
Print by: RJ Communication.
Printed in the United States of America
ISBN: 978-0-578-13347-8

Integrated Algebra
Table of Contents

Fundamental Concepts:

Operations:

Solving Equations

Evaluating:

Right triangle:

Statistics:

Real Numbers, Interval Notation & Sets

August 2012 – 9, 12

9. Which statement illustrates the additive identity property?

(1) $6 + 0 = 6$ (3) $4(6 + 3) = 4(6) + 4(3)$

(2) $-6 + 6 = 0$ (4) $(4 + 6) + 3 = 4 + (6 + 3)$

12. The length of a rectangle is 15 and its width is w. The perimeter of the rectangle is, *at most,* 50. Which inequality can be used to find the longest possible width?

(1) $30 + 2w < 50$ (3) $30 + 2w > 50$

(2) $30 + 2w \leq 50$ (4) $30 + 2w \geq 50$

June 2012 – 8, 17

8. If $A = \{0, 1, 3, 4, 6, 7\}$, $B = \{0, 2, 3, 5, 6\}$, and $C = \{0, 1, 4, 6, 7\}$, then $A \cap B \cap C$ is

(1) $\{0, 1, 2, 3, 4, 5, 6, 7\}$ (3) $\{0, 6\}$

(2) $\{0, 3, 6\}$ (4) $\{0\}$

17. Which interval notation describes the set
$S = \{x | 1 \leq x < 10\}$?

(1) [1,10]

(3) [1,10)

(2) (1,10]

(4) (1,10)

August 2011 – 3, 17

3. If the universal set is {pennies, nickels, dimes, quarters}, what is the complement of the set {nickels}?

(1) { }

(2) {pennies, quarters}

(3) {pennies, dimes, quarters}

(4) {pennies, nickels, dimes, quarters}

17. In interval notation, the set of all real numbers greater than −6 and less than or equal to 14 is represented by

(1) (−6, 14)

(3) (−6, 14]

(2) [−6, 14)

(4) [−6, 14]

June 2011 – 23, 28, 32

23. Given: $A = \{3, 6, 9, 12, 15\}$
$B = \{2, 4, 6, 8, 10, 12\}$

What is the union of sets A and B?

(1) $\{6\}$ (3) $\{2, 3, 4, 8, 9, 10, 15\}$

(2) $\{6, 12\}$ (4) $\{2, 3, 4, 6, 8, 9, 10, 12, 15\}$

28. Which notation describes $\{1, 2, 3\}$?

(1) $\{x \quad 1 \leq x < 3$, where x is an integer$\}$
(2) $\{x \quad 0 < x \leq 3$, where x is an integer$\}$
(3) $\{x \quad 1 < x < 3$, where x is an integer$\}$
(4) $\{x \quad 0 \leq x \leq 3$, where x is an integer$\}$

32. A method for solving $5(x - 2) - 2(x - 5) = 9$ is shown below. Identify the property used to obtain *each* of the two indicated steps.

$5(x - 2) - 2(x - 5) = 9$

(1) $5x - 10 - 2x + 10 = 9$ (1) _____

(2) $5x - 2x - 10 + 10 = 9$ (2) _____

        $3x + 0 = 9$

        $3x = 9$

        $x = 3$

August 2010 - 3, 9, 22

3.   What is the relationship between the independent and dependent variables in the scatter plot shown below?

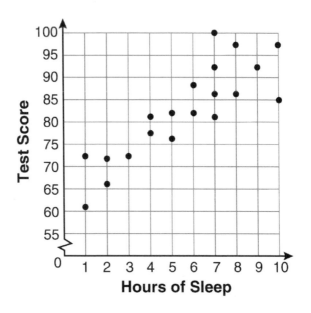

(1) undefined correlation   (3) positive correlation

(2) negative correlation   (4) no correlation

9. Which ratio represents sin *x* in the right triangle shown below?

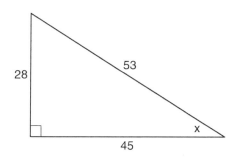

(1) $\dfrac{28}{53}$

(3) $\dfrac{45}{53}$

(2) $\dfrac{28}{45}$

(4) $\dfrac{53}{28}$

22. What is the slope of the line whose equation is $3x - 7y = 9$?

(1) $-\dfrac{3}{7}$

(3) $-\dfrac{7}{3}$

(2) $\dfrac{3}{7}$

(4) $\dfrac{7}{3}$

June 2010   1, 14, 21, 32

1. Given: Set $U = \{S, O, P, H, I, A\}$ Set $B = \{A, I, O\}$
If set B is a subset of set U, what is the complement of set B?

(1) $\{O, P, S\}$

(3) $\{A, H, P\}$

(2) $\{I, P, S\}$

(4) $\{H, P, S\}$

14. The algebraic expression $\frac{x-2}{x^2-9}$ is undefined when x is

(1) 0   (3) 3

(2) 2   (4) 9

21. Which interval notation represents the set of all numbers greater than or equal to 5 and less than 12?

(1) [5, 12)   (3) (5, 12)

(2) (5, 12]   (4) [5, 12]

32. Perform the indicated operation: $-6(a-7)$

State the name of the property used.

August 2009   12

12. Given: A = {All even integers from 2 to 20, inclusive} B = {10, 12, 14, 16, 18} What is the complement of set B within the universe of set A?

(1) {4, 6, 8}   (3) {4, 6, 8, 20}

(2) {2, 4, 6, 8}   (4) {2, 4, 6, 8, 20}

June 2009 16, 26, 30

16. Which value of n makes the expression $\dfrac{5n}{2n-1}$ undefined?

(1) 1

(3) $-\dfrac{1}{2}$

(2) 0

(4) $\dfrac{1}{2}$

26. What is the additive inverse of the expression $a - b$?

(1) $a + b$

(3) $-a + b$

(2) $a - b$

(4) $-a - b$

30. The set $\{11,12\}$ is equivalent to

(1) $\{x|11 < x < 12$, where x is an integer$\}$
(2) $\{x|11 < x \leq 12$, where x is an integer$\}$
(3) $\{x|10 \leq x < 12$, where x is an integer$\}$
(4) $\{x|10 < x \leq 12$, where x is an integer$\}$

Fractions and Percent

August 2012 – None

June 2012 – None

August 2011 - None

June 2011 - None

August 2010 – 7, 23

7. In a recent town election, 1,860 people voted for either candidate A or candidate B for the position of supervisor. If candidate A received 55% of the votes, how many votes did candidate B receive?

   (1) 186   (3) 1,023

   (2) 837   (4) 1,805

23. Corinne calculated the area of a paper plate to be 50.27 square inches. If the actual area of the plate is 55.42 square inches, what is the relative error in calculating the area, to the *nearest thousandth*?

   (1) 0.092   (3) 0.102

   (2) 0.093   (4) 0.103

June 2010 – None

August 2009 – None

June 2009 – None

Ratio & Proportion

August 2012 – 2, 10, 26

2.   A cell phone can receive 120 messages per minute. At this rate, how many messages can the phone receive in 150 seconds?

(1) 48   (3) 300

(2) 75   (4) 18,000

10.   Peter walked 8,900 feet from home to school.

> 1 mile = 5,280 feet

How far, to the *nearest tenth of a mile*, did he walk?

(1) 0.5   (3) 1.6

(2) 0.6   (4) 1.7

26.   What is the solution of $\dfrac{2}{x+1} = \dfrac{x+1}{2}$?

(1) -1 and -3 (3) 1 and -3

(2) -1 and 3   (4) 1 and 3

June 2012 – 1, 28

1.   In a baseball game, the ball traveled 350.7 feet in 4.2 seconds. What was the average speed of the ball, in feet per second?

(1) 83.5   (3) 354.9

(2) 177.5   (4) 1,472.9

28.   Elizabeth is baking chocolate chip cookies. A single batch uses $\frac{3}{4}$ teaspoon of vanilla. If Elizabeth is mixing the ingredients for five batches at the same time, how many tablespoons of vanilla will she use?

> **3 teaspoons = 1 tablespoon**

(1) $1\frac{1}{4}$ (3) $3\frac{3}{4}$

(2) $1\frac{3}{4}$ (4) $5\frac{3}{4}$

August 2011 – 1, 33

1.   The number of calories burned while jogging varies directly with the number of minutes spent jogging. If George burns 150 calories by jogging for 20 minutes, how many calories does he burn by jogging for 30 minutes?

(1) 100   (3) 200

(2) 180   (4) 225

33.   Mrs. Chen owns two pieces of property. The areas of the properties are 77,120 square feet and 33,500 square feet.

> **43,560 square feet = 1 acre**

Find the total number of acres Mrs. Chen owns, to the *nearest hundredth of an acre.*

June 2011 - 17

17. A hiker walked 12.8 miles from 9:00 a.m. to noon. He walked an additional 17.2 miles from 1:00 p.m. to 6:00 p.m. What is his average rate for the entire walk, in miles per hour?

    (1) 3.75   (3) 4.27

    (2) 3.86   (4) 7.71

August 2010 – 12, 32

12. Which value of x is the solution of $\dfrac{2x-3}{x-4} = \dfrac{2}{3}$?

    (1) $-\dfrac{1}{4}$ (3) -4

    (2) $\dfrac{1}{4}$ (4) 4

32. Joseph typed a 1,200-word essay in 25 minutes. At this rate, determine how many words he can type in 45 minutes.

June 2010 – 25

25. Steve ran a distance of 150 meters in $1\frac{1}{2}$ minutes. What is his speed in meters per hour?

    (1) 6   (3) 100

    (2) 60   (4) 6,000

August 2009 – None

June 2009 – 1, 11

1.   It takes Tammy 45 minutes to ride her bike 5 miles. At this rate, how long will it take her to ride 8 miles?

(1) 0.89 hour

(3) 48 minutes

(2) 1.125 hours

(4) 72 minutes

11.   If the speed of sound is 344 meters per second, what is the approximate speed of sound, in meters per hour?

> 60 seconds = 1 minute
> 60 minutes = 1 hour

(1) 20,640

(3) 123,840

(2) 41,280

(4) 1,238,400

<u>Rational Numbers & Monomials</u>

August 2012 – None

June 2012 – None

August 2011- None

June 2011 - 3

3.   The expression $\dfrac{12w^9y^3}{-3w^3y^3}$ is equivalent to

    (1) $-4w^6$ (3) $9w^6$

    (2) $-4w^3y$ (4) $9w^3y$

August 2010 – None

June 2010 – None

August 2009 - None

June 2009 - 3

3.   Which expression represents $\dfrac{27x^{18}y^5}{9x^6y}$ in simplest form?

    (1) $3x^{12}y^4$ (3) $18x^{12}y^4$

    (2) $3x^3y^5$ (4) $18x^3y^5$

Polynomials

August 2012 – 5, 22

5.   The sum of $3x^2 + 5x - 6$ and $-x^2 + 3x + 9$ is

(1) $2x^2 + 8x - 15$ (3) $2x^4 + 8x^2 + 3$

(2) $2x^2 + 8x + 3$ (4) $4x^2 + 2x - 15$

22.   Which expression is equivalent to

$$\frac{2x^6 - 18x^4 + 2x^2}{2x^2} \ ?$$

(1) $x^3 - 9x^2$ (3) $x^3 - 9x^2 + 1$

(2) $x^4 - 9x^2$ (4) $x^4 - 9x^2 + 1$

June 2012 – 3, 10, 26

3.   The quotient of $\dfrac{8x^5 - 2x^4 + 4x^3 - 6x^2}{2x^2}$ is

(1) $16x^7 - 4x^6 + 8x^5 - 12x^4$
(2) $4x^7 - x^6 + 2x^5 - 3x^4$
(3) $4x^3 - x^2 + 2x - 3x$
(4) $4x^3 - x^2 + 2x - 3$

10.   What is the product of $(3x + 2)$ and $(x - 7)$?

(1) $3x^2 - 14$ (3) $3x^2 - 19x - 14$

(2) $3x^2 - 5x - 14$ (4) $3x^2 - 23x - 14$

26. When $8x^2 + 3x + 2$ is subtracted from $9x^2 - 3x - 4$, the result is

(1) $x^2 - 2$ (3) $-x^2 + 6x + 6$

(2) $17x^2 - 2$ (4) $x^2 - 6x - 6$

August 2011 – None

June 2011 - 30

30. When $5x + 4y$ is subtracted from $5x - 4y$, the difference is

(1) 0 (3) $8y$

(2) $10x$ (4) $-8y$

August 2010 - None

June 2010 – 3

3. The sum of $4x^3 + 6x^2 + 2x - 3$ and $3x^3 + 3x^2 - 5x - 5$ is

(1) $7x^3 + 3x^2 - 3x - 8$ (3) $7x^3 + 9x^2 - 3x - 8$

(2) $7x^3 + 3x^2 + 7x + 2$ (4) $7x^6 + 9x^4 - 3x^2 - 8$

August 2009 – 3, 37

3. Which expression represents $(3x^2y^4)(4xy^2)$ in simplest form?

(1) $12x^2y^8$ (3) $12x^3y^8$

(2) $12x^2y^6$ (4) $12x^3y^6$

37. Express in simplest form: $\dfrac{2x^2-8x-42}{6x^2} \div \dfrac{x^2-9}{x^2-3x}$

June 2009 – 21, 23

21. Which expression represents $\dfrac{x^2-2x-15}{x^2+3x}$ in simplest form?

(1) -5 (3) $\dfrac{-2x-5}{x}$

(2) $\dfrac{x-5}{x}$ (4) $\dfrac{-2x-15}{3x}$

23. When $4x^2 + 7x - 5$ is subtracted from $9x^2 - 2x + 3$, the result is

(1) $5x^2 + 5x - 2$ (3) $-5x^2 + 5x - 2$

(2) $5x^2 - 9x + 8$ (4) $-5x^2 + 9x - 8$

<u>Roots and Radicals</u>

August 2012 – None

June 2012 – 36

36. Express $\dfrac{3\sqrt{75} + \sqrt{27}}{3}$ in simplest radical form.

August 2011 – 36

36. Express $\dfrac{16\sqrt{21}}{2\sqrt{7}} - 5\sqrt{12}$ in simplest radical form.

June 2011 - 6

6. What is $3\sqrt{250}$ expressed in simplest radical form?

    (1) $5\sqrt{10}$ (3) $15\sqrt{10}$

    (2) $8\sqrt{10}$ (4) $75\sqrt{10}$

August 2010 - 33

33. Express $-3\sqrt{48}$ in simplest radical form.

June 2010 – 8

8. The expression $\sqrt{72} - 3\sqrt{2}$ written in simplest radical form is

    (1) $5\sqrt{2}$ (3) $3\sqrt{2}$

    (2) $3\sqrt{6}$ (4) $\sqrt{6}$

August 2009 - 22

22. When $5\sqrt{20}$ is written in simplest radical form, the result is $k\sqrt{5}$.   What is the value of k?

    (1) 20   (3) 7

    (2) 10   (4) 4

June 2009 – 10

10. What is $\sqrt{32}$ expressed in simplest radical form?

    (1) $16\sqrt{2}$ (3) $4\sqrt{8}$

    (2) $4\sqrt{2}$ (4) $2\sqrt{8}$

__Algebraic Operations__ (including factoring)

August 2012 – 7, 32

7.   The expression $9a^2 - 64b^2$ is equivalent to

   (1) $(9a - 8b)(a + 8b)$ (3) $(3a - 8b)(3a + 8b)$

   (2) $(9a - 8b)(a - 8b)$ (4) $(3a - 8b)(3a - 8b)$

32.   Express the product of $\dfrac{x + 2}{2}$ and $\dfrac{4x + 20}{x^2 + 6x + 8}$ in simplest form.

June 2012 – 16, 20, 27

16.   Which expression represents $\dfrac{x^2 - 3x - 10}{x^2 - 25}$ in simplest form?

   (1) $\dfrac{2}{5}$ (3) $\dfrac{x - 2}{x - 5}$

   (2) $\dfrac{x + 2}{x + 5}$ (4) $\dfrac{-3x - 10}{-25}$

20. The expression $\dfrac{2x+13}{2x+6} - \dfrac{3x-6}{2x+6}$ is equivalent to

(1) $\dfrac{-x+19}{2(x+3)}$

(3) $\dfrac{5x+19}{2(x+3)}$

(2) $\dfrac{-x+7}{2(x+3)}$

(4) $\dfrac{5x+7}{4x+12}$

27. Factored completely, the expression $3x^3 - 33x^2 + 90x$ is equivalent to

(1) $3x(x^2 - 33x + 90)$

(3) $3x(x+5)(x+6)$

(2) $3x(x^2 - 11x + 30)$

(4) $3x(x-5)(x-6)$

August 2011 – 14, 29, 30

14. Which expression is equivalent to $-3x(x-4) - 2x(x+3)$?

(1) $-x^2 - 1$

(3) $-5x^2 - 6x$

(2) $-x^2 + 18x$

(4) $-5x^2 + 6x$

29. Which expression represents $36x^2 - 100y^6$ factored completely?

(1) $2(9x + 25y^3)(9x - 25y^3)$

(2) $4(3x + 5y^3)(3x - 5y^3)$

(3) $(6x + 10y^3)(6x - 10y^3)$

(4) $(18x + 50y^3)(18x - 50y^3)$

30. What is the quotient of $\dfrac{x}{x+4}$ divided by $\dfrac{2x}{x^2-16}$?

(1) $\dfrac{2}{x-4}$

(3) $\dfrac{2x^2}{x^2-16}$

(2) $\dfrac{2x^2}{x-4}$

(4) $\dfrac{x-4}{2}$

June 2011 – 1, 5, 25, 29

1. The expression $x^2 - 36y^2$ is equivalent to

(1) $(x - 6y)(x - 6y)$

(3) $(x + 6y)(x - 6y)$

(2) $(x - 18y)(x - 18y)$

(4) $(x + 18y)(x - 18y)$

5. What are the factors of the expression $x^2 + x - 20$?

(1) $(x + 5)$ and $(x + 4)$

(3) $(x - 5)$ and $(x + 4)$

(2) $(x + 5)$ and $(x - 4)$

(4) $(x - 5)$ and $(x - 4)$

25. For which set of values of x is the algebraic expression $\dfrac{x^2-16}{x^2-4x-12}$ undefined?

(1) $\{-6, 2\}$　　　　　　　　(3) $\{-4, 4\}$

(2) $\{-4, 3\}$　　　　　　　　(4) $\{-2, 6\}$

29. What is $\dfrac{7}{12x} - \dfrac{y}{6x^2}$ expressed in simplest form?

(1) $\dfrac{7-y}{6x}$　　　　　　　　(3) $-\dfrac{7y}{12x^2}$

(2) $\dfrac{7-y}{12x-6x^2}$　　　　　　(4) $\dfrac{7x-2y}{12x^2}$

August 2010 – 8, 27, 31

8. Which expression is equivalent to $121 - x^2$?

(1) $(x - 11)(x - 11)$　　　　　(3) $(11 - x)(11 + x)$

(2) $(x + 11)(x - 11)$　　　　　(4) $(11 - x)(11 - x)$

27. What is $\dfrac{2+x}{5x} - \dfrac{x-2}{5x}$ expressed in simplest form?

(1) 0　　　　　　　　　　(3) $\dfrac{4}{5x}$

(2) $\dfrac{2}{5}$　　　　　　　　　(4) $\dfrac{2x+4}{5x}$

31. Express in simplest form: $\dfrac{45a^4b^3 - 90a^3b}{15a^2b}$

June 2010 – 18, 24, 27, 37

18. Which expression represents $\dfrac{-14a^2c^8}{7a^3c^2}$ in simplest form?

(1) $-2ac^4$

(3) $\dfrac{-2c^4}{a}$

(2) $-2ac^6$

(4) $\dfrac{-2c^6}{a}$

24. What is the sum of $\dfrac{-x+7}{2x+4}$ and $\dfrac{2x+5}{2x+4}$?

(1) $\dfrac{x+12}{2x+4}$

(3) $\dfrac{x+12}{4x+8}$

(2) $\dfrac{3x+12}{2x+4}$

(4) $\dfrac{3x+12}{4x+8}$

27. Factored completely, the expression $3x2 - 3x - 18$ is equivalent to

(1) $3(x2 - x - 6)$

(3) $(3x - 9)(x + 2)$

(2) $3(x - 3)(x + 2)$

(4) $(3x + 6)(x - 3)$

37. Express in simplest form:

$$\dfrac{x^2 + 9x + 14}{x^2 - 49} \div \dfrac{3x + 6}{x^2 + x - 56}$$

August 2009 – 1, 2, 17, 18

1. If h represents a number, which equation is a correct translation of

   "Sixty more than 9 times a number is 375"?

   (1) $9h = 375$ (3) $9h - 60 = 375$

   (2) $9h + 60 = 375$ (4) $60h + 9 = 375$

2. Which expression is equivalent to $9x^2 - 16$?

   (1) $(3x + 4)(3x - 4)$ (3) $(3x + 8)(3x - 8)$

   (2) $(3x - 4)(3x - 4)$ (4) $(3x - 8)(3x - 8)$

17. What is the sum of $\dfrac{3}{2x}$ and $\dfrac{4}{3x}$ expressed in simplest form?

   (1) $\dfrac{12}{6x^2}$ (3) $\dfrac{7}{5x}$

   (2) $\dfrac{17}{6x}$ (4) $\dfrac{17}{12x}$

18. Which value of x makes the expression
$$\frac{x^2 - 9}{x^2 + 7x + 10} \text{ undefined?}$$

(1) -5 (3) 3

(2) 2   (4) -3

June 2009 – 29, 32

29. What is $\dfrac{6}{4a} - \dfrac{2}{3a}$ expressed in simplest form?

(1) $\dfrac{4}{a}$ (3) $\dfrac{8}{7a}$

(2) $\dfrac{5}{6a}$ (4) $\dfrac{10}{12a}$

32. Factor completely: $4x^3 - 36x$

Functions

August 2012 – None

June 2012 – 9

9. Which graph represents a function?

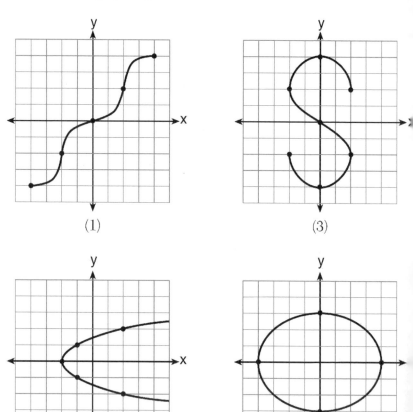

(1)

(2)

(3)

(4)

August 2011 – 34

34. On the set of axes below, graph and label the equations $y = |x|$ and $y = 3|x|$ for the interval $-3 \leq x \leq 3$.

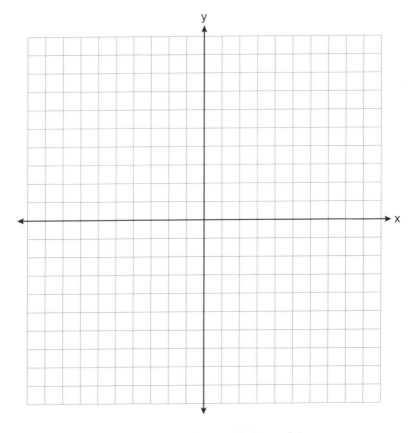

Explain how changing the coefficient of the absolute value from 1 to 3 affects the graph.

June 2011 – 11, 16

11. Which type of function is represented by the graph shown below?

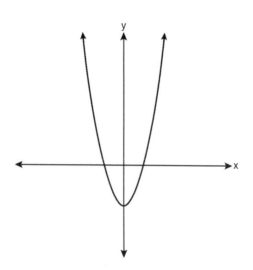

(1) absolute value (3) linear

(2) exponential (4) quadratic

16. Which set of ordered pairs represents a function?

(1) $\{(0,4), (2,4), (2,5)\}$
(2) $\{(6,0), (5,0), (4,0)\}$
(3) $\{(4,1), (6,2), (6,3), (5,0)\}$
(4) $\{(0,4), (1,4), (0,5), (1,5)\}$

August 2010 – None

June 2010 – 13, 35

13. Which graph represents a function?

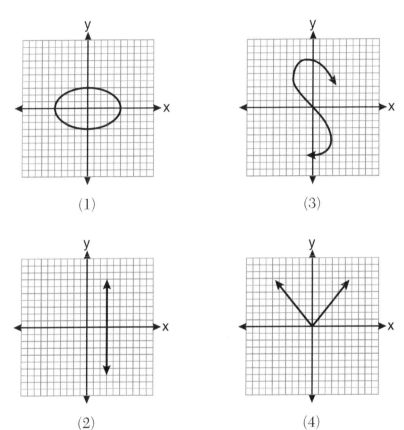

35. Graph and label the following equations on the set of axes below.

$$y = |x|$$

$$y = \left| \frac{1}{2} x \right|$$

Explain how *decreasing* the coefficient of x affects the graph of the equation $y = |x|$.

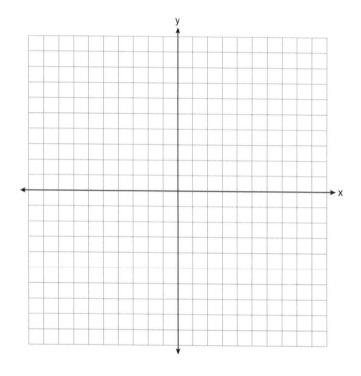

August 2009 – 19, 25

19. Which relation is *not* a function?

(1) $\{(1,5), (2,6), (3,6), (4,7)\}$

(2) $\{(4,7), (2,1), (-3,6), (3,4)\}$

(3) $\{(-1,6), (1,3), (2,5), (1,7)\}$

(4) $\{(-1,2), (0,5), (5,0), (2,-1)\}$

25. Which equation is represented by the graph below?

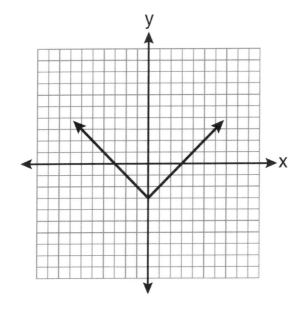

(1) $y = x^2 - 3$ (3) $y = |x| - 3$

(2) $y = (x - 3)^2$ (4) $y = |x - 3|$

June 2009 – 19

19. Which statement is true about the relation shown on the graph below?

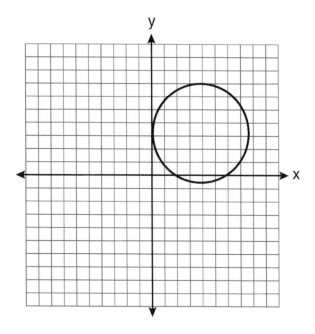

(1) It is a function because there exists one *x*- coordinate for each *y*-coordinate.

(2) It is a function because there exists one *y*-coordinate for each *x*-coordinate.

(3) It is *not* a function because there are multiple *y*-values for a given *x*-value.

(4) It is *not* a function because there are multiple *x*-values for a given *y*-value.

Linear Equations & Inequalities

August 2012 – 3, 27

3. The value of y in the equation
$0.06y + 200 = 0.03y + 350$ is

(1) 500   (3) 5,000

(2) $1,666.\overline{6}$ (4) $18,333.\overline{3}$

27. The total score in a football game was 72 points. The winning team scored 12 points more than the losing team. How many points did the winning team score?

(1) 30   (3) 54

(2) 42   (4) 60

June 2012 – 11, 38

11. If five times a number is less than 55, what is the greatest possible integer value of the number?

(1) 12   (3) 10

(2) 11   (4) 9

38. Solve algebraically for x:

$$3(x + 1) - 5x = 12 - (6x - 7)$$

August 2011 – 21, 39

21.   What is the solution of the inequality
$-6x - 17 \geq 8x + 25$?

(1) $x \geq 3$ (3) $x \geq -3$

(2) $x \leq 3$ (4) $x \leq -3$

39.   Solve for m: $\dfrac{m}{5} + \dfrac{3(m-1)}{2} = 2(m-3)$

June 2011 – 26, 35, 37

26.   Michael is 25 years younger than his father.
The sum of their ages is 53.
What is Michael's age?

(1) 14   (3) 28

(2) 25   (4) 39

35.   Chelsea has $45 to spend at the fair. She
spends $20 on admission and $15 on snacks.
She wants to play a game that costs $0.65 per
game. Write an inequality to find the maximum
number of times, x, Chelsea can play the game.

Using this inequality, determine the maximum
number of times she can play the game.

37.   Solve algebraically for x: $\dfrac{3}{4} = \dfrac{-(x+11)}{4x} + \dfrac{1}{2x}$

August 2010 – 2

2.   What is the solution of $3(2m - 1) \le 4m + 7$?

   (1) $m \le 5$ (3) $m \le 4$

   (2) $m \ge 5$ (4) $m \ge 4$

June 2010 – 19, 28, 34

19.   Which value of x is the solution of $\frac{x}{3} + \frac{x+1}{2} = x$?

   (1)   1   (3)   3

   (2) −1   (4) −3

28.   Which quadrant will be completely shaded
in the graph of the inequality $y \le 2x$?

   (1) Quadrant I   (3) Quadrant III

   (2) Quadrant II   (4) Quadrant IV

34.   Given: A = {18, 6, −3, −12}

   Determine all elements of set A that are in the
solution of the inequality $\frac{2}{3}x + 3 < -2x - 7$.

August 2009 – 4, 9, 13

4 . An online music club has a one-time registration fee of $13.95 and charges $0.49 to buy each song. If Emma has $50.00 to join the club and buy songs, what is the maximum number of songs she can buy?

(1) 73   (3) 130

(2) 74   (4) 131

9. Solve for x: $\frac{3}{5}(x + 2) = x - 4$

(1) 8   (3) 15

(2) 13   (4) 23

13. Which value of x is in the solution set of the inequality $-2(x - 5) < 4$?

(1) 0   (3) 3

(2) 2   (4) 5

June 2009 – 7, 14, 20

7. Which value of x is the solution of the equation $\frac{2x}{3} + \frac{x}{6} = 5$?

(1) 6   (3) 15

(2) 10   (4) 30

14. Which value of x is in the solution set of $\frac{4}{3}x + 5 < 17$?

(1) 8   (3) 12

(2) 9   (4) 16

20. Which graph represents the solution of $3y - 9 \le 6x$?

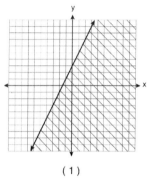

(1)

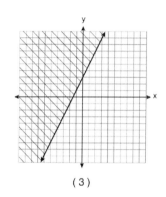

(3)

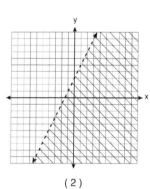

(2)

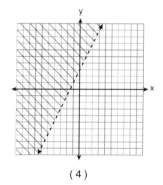

(4)

Solving Literal Equations & Formulas

August 2012 – 30

30. The formula for the volume of a pyramid is $V = \frac{1}{3}Bh$. What is h expressed in terms of B and V?

(1) $h = \frac{1}{3}VB$

(3) $h = \frac{3V}{B}$

(2) $h = \frac{V}{3B}$

(4) $h = 3VB$

June 2012 – 15

15. If $k = am + 3mx$, the value of m in terms of a, k, and x can be expressed as

(1) $\frac{k}{a + 3x}$

(3) $\frac{k - am}{3x}$

(2) $\frac{k - 3mx}{a}$

(4) $\frac{k - a}{3x}$

August 2011 – 31

31. Solve for c in terms of a and b: $bc + ac = ab$

June 2011 – None

August 2010 – None

June 2010 – 23

23.   A formula used for calculating velocity is $v = \frac{1}{2}at^2$. What is a expressed in terms of v and t?

(1) $a = \frac{2v}{t}$ (3) $a = \frac{v}{t}$

(2) $a = \frac{2v}{t^2}$ (4) $a = \frac{v}{2t^2}$

August 2009 – None

June 2009 – 13

13.   If $a + ar = b + r$, the value of a in terms of b and r can be expressed as

(1) $\frac{b}{r} + 1$ (3) $\frac{b+r}{1+r}$

(2) $\frac{1+b}{r}$ (4) $\frac{1+b}{r+b}$

Evaluating Formulas & Algebraic Expressions

August 2012 – 20, 25

20. What is the value of $\left| \dfrac{4(-6) + 18}{4!} \right|$?

(1) $\dfrac{1}{4}$

(3) 12

(2) $-\dfrac{1}{4}$

(4) -12

25. The expression $\dfrac{14 + x}{x^2 - 4}$ is undefined when x is

(1) -14, only

(3) -2 or 2

(2) 2, only

(4) $-14, -2,$ or 2

June 2012 – None

August 2011 – 10, 13

10. Which algebraic expression represents 15 less than x divided by 9?

(1) $\dfrac{x}{9} - 15$

(3) $15 - \dfrac{x}{9}$

(2) $9x - 15$

(4) $15 - 9x$

13. What is the value of the expression $-3x^2y + 4x$ when $x = -4$ and $y = 2$?

(1) -112 (3) 80

(2) -80 (4) 272

June 2011 – 19, 21

19. Which verbal expression can be represented by $2(x - 5)$?

(1) 5 less than 2 times x
(2) 2 multiplied by x less than 5
(3) twice the difference of x and 5
(4) the product of 2 and x, decreased by 5

21. An example of an algebraic expression is

(1) $y = mx + b$ (3) $2x + 3y \leq 18$

(2) $3x + 4y - 7$ (4) $(x + y)(x - y) = 25$

August 2010 – 30

30. An example of an algebraic expression is

(1) $x + 2$ (3) $y < x + 2$

(2) $y = x + 2$ (4) $y = x^2 + 2x$

August 2009 – 23

23. What is the value of the expression $|-5x + 12|$ when $x = 5$?

(1) -37 (3) 13

(2) -13 (4) 37

June 2009 – 6

6. The sign shown below is posted in front of a roller coaster ride at the Wadsworth County Fairgrounds.

> All riders **MUST** be
> At least 48 inches tall.

If h represents the height of a rider in inches, what is a correct translation of the statement on this sign?

(1) $h < 48$ (3) $h \leq 48$

(2) $h > 48$ (4) $h \geq 48$

Properties of Exponents and Scientific Notation

August 2012 – 31

31. State the value of the expression

$$\frac{(4.1 \times 10^2)(2.4 \times 10^3)}{(1.5 \times 10^7)}$$ in scientific notation.

June 2012 – 19

19. What is one-third of 3^6?

(1) 1^2 (3) 3^5

(2) 3^2 (4) 9^6

August 2011 – None

June 2011 - 27

27. What is the product of (6×10^3), (4.6×10^5), and (2×10^{-2}) expressed in scientific notation?

(1) 55.2×10^6 (3) 55.2×10^7

(2) 5.52×10^7 (4) 5.52×10^{10}

August 2010 - 6

6. The quotient of (9.2×10^6) and (2.3×10^2) expressed in scientific notation is

    (1) 4,000   (3) 4×10^3

    (2) 40,000   (4) 4×10^4

June 2010 – None

August 2009 – None

June 2009 - 27

27. What is the product of 12 and 4.2×10^6 expressed in scientific notation?

    (1) 50.4×10^6 (3) 5.04×10^6

    (2) 50.4×10^7 (4) 5.04×10^7

Exponential Functions

August 2012 – 11, 33

11. Is the equation $A = 21000(1 - 0.12)^t$ a model of exponential growth or exponential decay, and what is the rate (percent) of change per time period?

(1) exponential growth and 12%
(2) exponential growth and 88%
(3) exponential decay and 12%
(4) exponential decay and 88%

33. On the set of axes below, graph $y = 3^x$ over the interval $-1 \le x \le 2$.

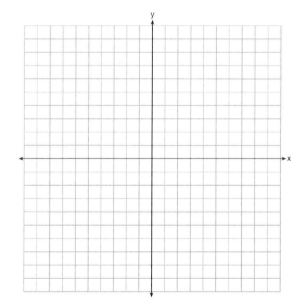

June 2012 – 29

29. A car depreciates (loses value) at a rate of 4.5% annually. Greg purchased a car for $12,500. Which equation can be used to determine the value of the car, V, after 5 years?

(1) $V = 12,500(0.55)^5$ (3) $V = 12,500(1.045)^5$

(2) $V = 12,500(0.955)^5$ (4) $V = 12,500(1.45)^5$

August 2011 – 24

24. The current student population of the Brentwood Student Center is 2,000. The enrollment at the center increases at a rate of 4% each year. To the *nearest whole number*, what will the student population   be closest to in 3 years?

(1) 2,240   (3) 5,488

(2) 2,250   (4) 6,240

June 2011 - 24

24. The value of a car purchased for $20,000 decreases at a rate of 12% per year. What will be the value of the car after 3 years?

(1) $12,800.00   (3) $17,600.00

(2) $13,629.44   (4) $28,098.56

August 2010 – 25

25. Which graph represents an exponential equation?

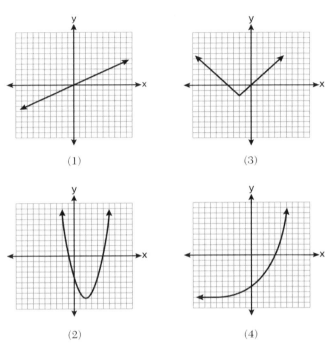

(1)

(3)

(2)

(4)

June 2010 – 30

30. The value, y, of a $15,000 investment over x years is represented by the equation

$$y = 15000(1.2)^{\frac{x}{3}}$$ What is the profit (interest) on a 6-year investment?

(1) $6,600

(3) $21,600

(2) $10,799

(4) $25,799

August 2009 – 29

29. Cassandra bought an antique dresser for $500. If the value of her dresser increases 6% annually, what will be the value of Cassandra's dresser at the end of 3 years to the *nearest dollar*?

(1) $415   (3) $596

(2) $590   (4) $770

June 2009 – 35

35. A bank is advertising that new customers can open a savings account with a $3\frac{3}{4}\%$ interest rate compounded annually. Robert invests $5,000 in an account at this rate. If he makes no additional deposits or withdrawals on his account, find the amount of money he will have, to the *nearest cent*, after three years.

Graphing Linear Equations

August 2012 – 17, 19, 23

17. Which set of coordinates is a solution of the equation $2x - y = 11$?

(1) $(-6, -1)$ (3) $(0, 11)$

(2) $(-1, 9)$ (4) $(2, -7)$

19. Which equation represents a line that has a slope of $\dfrac{3}{2}$ and passes through the point $(2,1)$?

(1) $3y = 4x - 5$ (3) $4y = 3x - 2$

(2) $3y = 4x + 2$ (4) $4y = 3x + 5$

23. In a given linear equation, the value of the independent variable decreases at a constant rate while the value of the dependent variable increases at a constant rate.
The slope of this line is

(1) positive   (3) zero

(2) negative   (4) undefined

June 2012 – 12, 21

12. The line represented by the equation $2y - 3x = 4$ has a slope of

(1) $-\dfrac{3}{2}$ (3) 3

(2) 2   (4) $\dfrac{3}{2}$

21. Which equation is represented by the graph below?

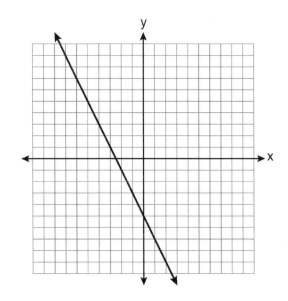

(1) $2y + x = 10$ (3) $-2y = 10x - 4$

(2) $y - 2x = -5$ (4) $2y = -4x - 10$

August 2011 – 8, 15

8. Which equation represents the line that passes through the point (1,5) and has a slope of −2?

(1) $y = -2x + 7$ (3) $y = 2x - 9$

(2) $y = -2x + 11$ (4) $y = 2x + 3$

15. The data in the table below are graphed, and the slope is examined.

x	y
0.5	9.0
1	8.75
1.5	8.5
2	8.25
2.5	8.0

The rate of change represented in this table can be described as

(1) negative   (3) undefined

(2) positive   (4) zero

June 2011 – 10, 12

10.   What is the slope of the line passing through the points $(-2,4)$ and $(3,6)$?

(1) $-\dfrac{5}{2}$ (3) $\dfrac{2}{5}$

(2) $-\dfrac{2}{5}$ (4) $\dfrac{5}{2}$

12.   Which equation represents a line parallel to the y-axis?

(1) $y = x$ (3) $x = -y$

(2) $y = 3$ (4) $x = -4$

August 2010 – 5, 14, 16, 29

5.   What is the slope of the line passing through the points A and B, as shown on the graph below?

(1) -3 (3) 3

(2) $-\dfrac{1}{3}$ (4) $\dfrac{1}{3}$

14.   Which equation represents a line parallel to the y-axis?

(1) $x = y$ (3) $y = 4$

(2) $x = 4$ (4) $y = x + 4$

16. Which point lies on the line whose equation is $2x - 3y = 9$?

(1) $(-1,-3)$ (3) $(0, 3)$

(2) $(-1, 3)$ (4) $(0,-3)$

29. What is an equation of the line that passes through the points $(1, 3)$ and $(8, 5)$?

(1) $y + 1 = \frac{2}{7}(x + 3)$ (3) $y - 1 = \frac{2}{7}(x + 3)$

(2) $y - 5 = \frac{2}{7}(x - 8)$ (4) $y + 5 = \frac{2}{7}(x - 8)$

June 2010 – 4, 7, 15

4. What is the slope of the line that passes through the points $(3, 5)$ and $(-2, 2)$?

(1) $\frac{1}{5}$ (3) $\frac{5}{3}$

(2) $\frac{3}{5}$ (4) 5

7. Which linear equation represents a line containing the point $(1, 3)$?

(1) $x + 2y = 5$ (3) $2x + y = 5$

(2) $x - 2y = 5$ (4) $2x - y = 5$

15. The graphs of the equations $y = 2x - 7$ and $y - kx = 7$ are parallel when k equals

(1) −2

(3) −7

(2) 2

(4) 7

August 2009 – 11, 15, 27

11. Which equation represents a line parallel to the x-axis?

(1) $y = -5$

(3) $x = 3$

(2) $y = -5x$

(4) $x = 3y$

15. What is the slope of the line that passes through the points $(-5, 4)$ and $(15, -4)$?

(1) $-\frac{2}{5}$

(3) $-\frac{5}{2}$

(2) 0

(4) undefined

27. What is an equation of the line that passes through the point $(3, -1)$ and has a slope of 2?

(1) $y = 2x + 5$

(3) $y = 2x - 4$

(2) $y = 2x - 1$

(4) $y = 2x - 7$

June 2009 – 22

22. What is an equation of the line that passes through the point (4,−6) and has a slope of −3?

(1) $y = -3x + 6$ (3) $y = -3x + 10$

(2) $y = -3x - 6$ (4) $y = -3x + 14$

Graphing: Systems, Linear, and Inequalities

August 2012 – 1, 39

1. A system of equations is graphed on the set of axes below.

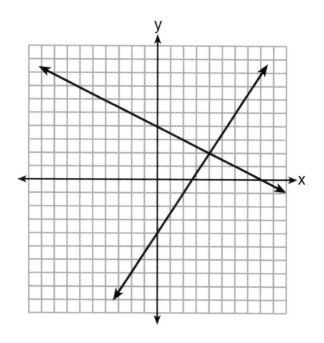

The solution of this system is

(1) (0, 4)   (3) (4, 2)

(2) (2, 4)   (4) (8, 0)

39. On the set of axes below, graph the following system of inequalities.

$$y + x \geq 3$$
$$5x - 2y > 10$$

State the coordinates of *one* point that satisfies $y + x \geq 3$, but does *not* satisfy $5x - 2y > 10$.

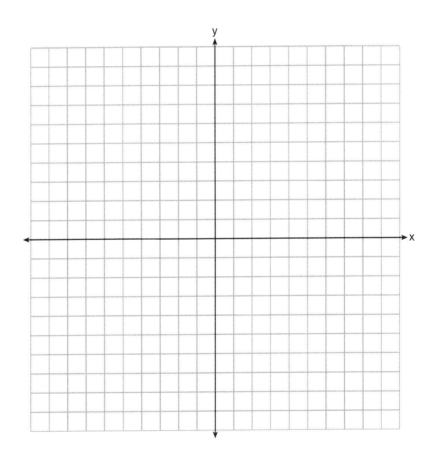

June 2012 – 22, 31

22.   Which coordinates represent a point in the solution set of the system of inequalities shown below?

$$y \leq \frac{1}{2}x + 13$$
$$4x + 2y = 3$$

(1) $(-4, 1)$ (3) $(1, -4)$

(2) $(-2, 2)$ (4) $(2, -2)$

31.   Solve the following system of equations algebraically for y:

$$2x + 2y = 9$$
$$2x - y = 3$$

August 2011 – 9, 27

9.   What is the solution of the system of equations $2x - 5y = 11$ and $-2x + 3y = -9$?

(1) $(-3,-1)$ (3) $(3,-1)$

(2) $(-1,3)$ (4) $(3,1)$

27. Which ordered pair is in the solution set of the system of inequalities shown in the graph below?

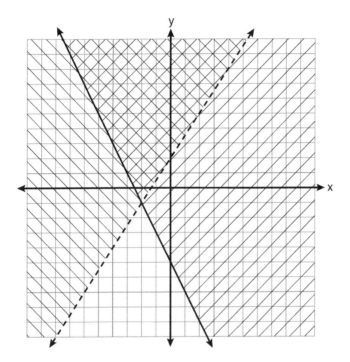

(1) (−2,−1)   (3) (−2,−4)

(2) (−2,2)   (4) (2,−2)

June 2011 – 39

39. Solve the following system of inequalities graphically on the set of axes below.

$$3x + y < 7$$

$$y \geq \frac{2}{3}x - 4$$

State the coordinates of a point in the solution set.

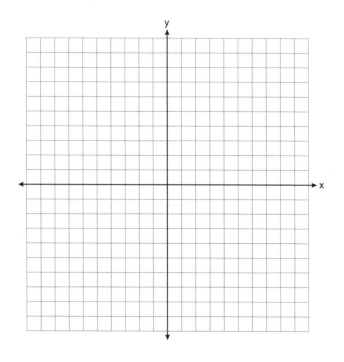

August 2010 – 21, 37

21. What is the value of the *y*-coordinate of the solution to the system of equations $2x + y = 8$ and $x - 3y = -3$?

(1) −2 (3) 3

(2) 2 (4) −3

37. On the set of axes below, solve the following system of inequalities graphically.

$$y < 2x + 1$$
$$y \geq -\frac{1}{3}x + 4$$

State the coordinates of a point in the solution set.

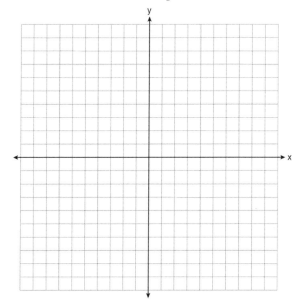

June 2010 – 10, 12

10. Which ordered pair is in the solution set of the system of linear inequalities graphed below?

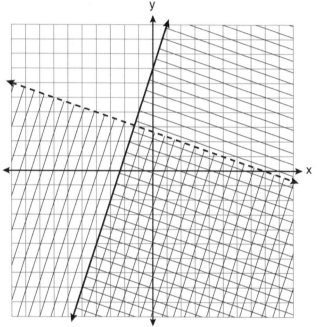

(1) $(1, -4)$ (3) $(5, 3)$

(2) $(-5, 7)$ (4) $(-7, -2)$

12. What is the solution of the system of equations $c + 3d = 8$ and $c = 4d - 6$?

(1) $c = -14, d = -2$ (3) $c = 2, d = 2$

(2) $c = -2, d = 2$ (4) $c = 14, d = -2$

August 2009 – 20, 38

20.   What is the value of the *y*-coordinate of the solution
to the system   of equations $x - 2y = 1$ and $x + 4y = 7$?

(1) 1   (3) 3

(2) −1   (4) 4

38.   On the grid below, solve the system of equations
graphically for *x* and *y*.

$$4x - 2y = 10$$

$$y = -2x - 1$$

June 2009 – 12, 25

12. The sum of two numbers is 47, and their difference is 15. What is the larger number?

(1) 16

(3) 32

(2) 31

(4) 36

25. What is the value of the y-coordinate of the solution to the system of equations $x + 2y = 9$ and $x - y = 3$?

(1) 6

(3) 3

(2) 2

(4) 5

<u>Mathematical Modeling</u>

August 2012 – 6, 12, 15

6.   Jason's part-time job pays him $155 a week.
     If he has already saved $375, what is the minimum
     number of weeks he needs to work in order to have
     enough money to buy a dirt bike for $900?

     (1) 8   (3) 3

     (2) 9   (4) 4

12. The length of a rectangle is 15 and its width is w.
     The perimeter of the rectangle is, *at most,* 50.
     Which inequality can be used to find the longest
     possible width?

     (1) $30 + 2w < 50$ (3) $30 + 2w > 50$

     (2) $30 + 2w \leq 50$ (4) $30 + 2w \geq 50$

15. A correct translation of "six less than twice
     the value of x" is

     (1) $2x < 6$ (3) $6 < 2x$

     (2) $2x - 6$ (4) $6 - 2x$

June 2012 – 4, 25

4. Marcy determined that her father's age is four less than three times her age. If x represents Marcy's age, which expression represents her father's age?

(1) $3x - 4$ (3) $4x - 3$

(2) $3(x - 4)$ (4) $4 - 3x$

25. If n is an odd integer, which equation can be used to find three consecutive odd integers whose sum is -3?

(1) $n + (n + 1) + (n + 3) = -3$

(2) $n + (n + 1) + (n + 2) = -3$

(3) $n + (n + 2) + (n + 4) = -3$

(4) $n + (n + 2) + (n + 3) = -3$

August 2011 – 7, 19

7. The ninth grade class at a local high school needs to purchase a park permit for $250.00 for their upcoming class picnic. Each ninth grader attending the picnic pays $0.75. Each guest pays $1.25. If 200 ninth graders attend the picnic, which inequality can be used to determine the number of guests, x, needed to cover the cost of the permit?

(1) $0.75x - (1.25)(200) \geq 250.00$

(2) $0.75x + (1.25)(200) \geq 250.00$

(3) $(0.75)(200) - 1.25x \geq 250.00$

(4) $(0.75)(200) + 1.25x \geq 250.00$

19.   Ben has four more than twice as many CDs as Jake.
        If they have a total of 31 CDs, how   many CDs does
        Jake have?

    (1) 9   (3) 14

    (2) 13   (4) 22

August 2010 – 11

11.   The width of a rectangle is 3 less than twice the
        length, x. If the area of the rectangle is 43 square
        feet, which equation can be used to find the length,
        in feet?

    (1) $2x(x - 3) = 43$ (3) $2x + 2(2x - 3) = 43$

    (2) $x(3 - 2x) = 43$ (4) $x(2x - 3) = 43$

June 2010 – 16

16.   Which verbal expression is represented by
        $\frac{1}{2}(n - 3)$?

    (1) one-half n decreased by 3

    (2) one-half n subtracted from 3

    (3) the difference of one-half n and 3

    (4) one-half the difference of n and 3

August 2009 – None

June 2009 – 4, 17

4.   Marie currently has a collection of 58 stamps.
       If she buys s stamps each week for w weeks,
       which expression represents the total
       number of stamps she will have?

    (1) $58sw$ (3) $58s + w$

    (2) $58 + sw$ (4) $58 + s + w$

17.   At Genesee High School, the sophomore class
       has 60 more students than the freshman class.
       The junior class has 50 fewer students than
       twice the students in the freshman class. The
       senior class is three times as large as the freshman
       class. If there are a total of 1,424 students at
       Genesee High School, how many students are in
       the freshman class?

    (1) 202   (3) 235

    (2) 205   (4) 236

Best Fit

August 2012 – 4, 8

4. The scatter plot shown below represents a relationship between x and y.

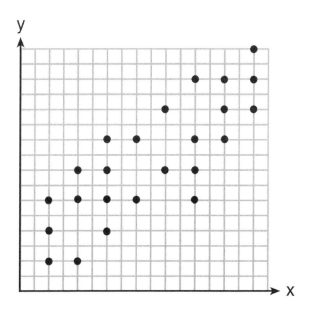

This type of relationship is

(1) a positive correlation (3) a zero correlation

(2) a negative correlation (4) not able to be determined

8.   The scatter plot below shows the profit, by month,
For a new company for the first year of operation.
Kate drew a line of best fit, as shown in the diagram.

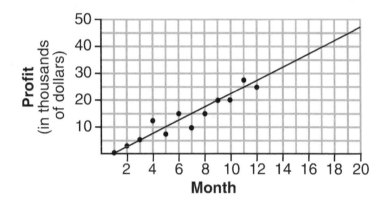

Using this line, what is the best estimate for
profit in the 18th month?

(1) $35,000   (3) $42,500

(2) $37,750   (4) $45,000

June 2012 – 5

5   A set of data is graphed on the scatter plot below.

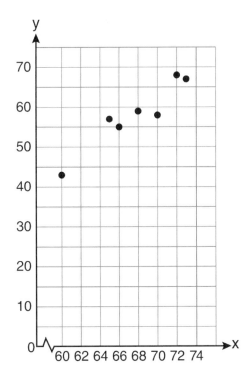

This scatter plot shows

(1) no correlation

(2) positive correlation

(3) negative correlation

(4) undefined correlation

August 2011 – 2

2. The scatter plot below represents the relationship between the number of peanuts a student eats and the student's bowling score.

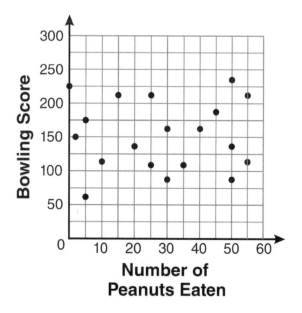

Which conclusion about the scatter plot is valid?

(1) There is almost no relationship between eating peanuts and bowling score.

(2) Students who eat more peanuts have higher bowling scores.

(3) Students who eat more peanuts have lower bowling scores.

(4) No bowlers eat peanuts.

June 2011 – 15, 22

15. The maximum height and speed of various roller coasters in North America are shown in the table below.

Maximum Speed, in mph, (x)	45	50	54	60	65	70
Maximum Height, in feet, (y)	63	80	105	118	141	107

Which graph represents a correct scatter plot of the data?

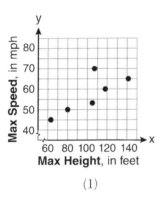

(1)

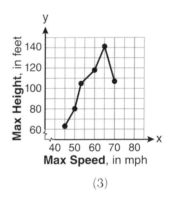

(3)

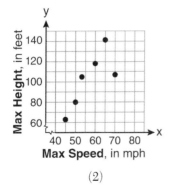

(2)

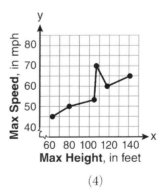

(4)

22. A study showed that a decrease in the cost of carrots led to an increase in the number of carrots sold. Which statement best describes this relationship?

(1) positive correlation and a causal relationship

(2) negative correlation and a causal relationship

(3) positive correlation and not a causal relationship

(4) negative correlation and not a causal relationship

August 2010 – 1

1.   The school store did a study comparing the cost of a sweatshirt with the number of sweatshirts sold. The price was changed several times and the numbers of sweatshirts sold were recorded. The data are shown in the table below.

Cost of Sweatshirt	$10	$25	$15	$20	$5
Number Sold	9	6	15	11	14

Which scatter plot represents the data?

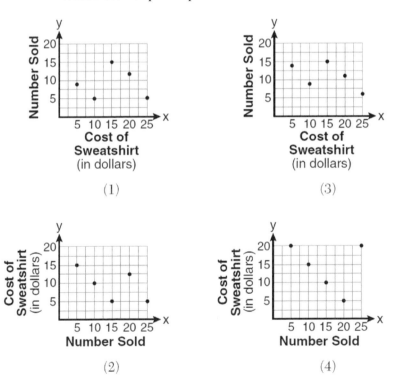

(1)

(3)

(2)

(4)

June 2010 – 36

36. Megan and Bryce opened a new store called the Donut Pit. Their goal is to reach a profit of $20,000 in their 18th month of business. The table and scatter plot below represent the profit, P, in thousands of dollars, that they made during the first 12 months.

t (months)	1	2	3	4	5	6	7	8	9	10	11	12
P (profit, in thousands of dollars)	3.0	2.5	4.0	5.0	6.5	5.5	7.0	6.0	7.5	7.0	9.0	9.5

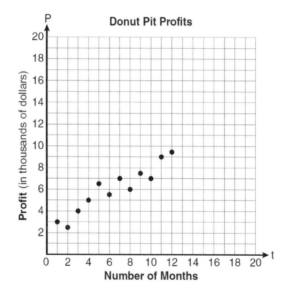

Draw a reasonable line of best fit.

Using the line of best fit, predict whether Megan and Bryce will reach their goal in the 18th month of their business. Justify your answer.

August 2009 – 30

30.   The number of hours spent on math homework
each week and the final exam grades for twelve
students in Mr. Dylan's algebra class are
plotted below.

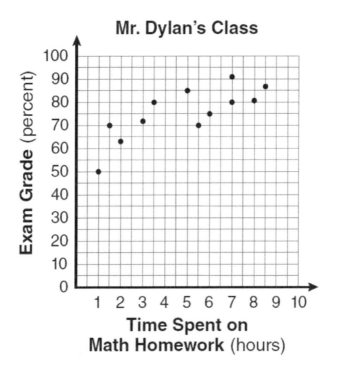

Based on a line of best fit, which exam grade is the
best prediction for a student who spends about 4
hours on math homework each week?

(1) 62   (3) 82

(2) 72   (4) 92

June 2009 – 36

36. The table below shows the number of prom tickets sold over a ten-day period.

Prom Ticket Sales

Day (x)	1	2	5	7	10
Number of Prom Tickets Sold (y)	30	35	55	60	70

Plot these data points on the coordinate grid below. Use a consistent and appropriate scale. Draw a reasonable line of best fit and write its equation.

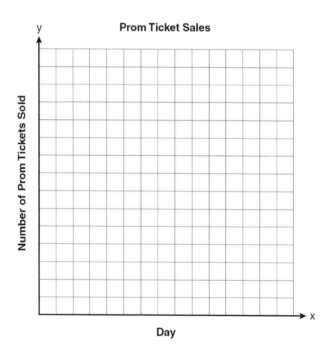

Quadratics, Algebraic and Graphical Solutions

August 2012 – 14, 18

14. What are the coordinates of the vertex and the equation of the axis of symmetry of the parabola shown in the graph below?

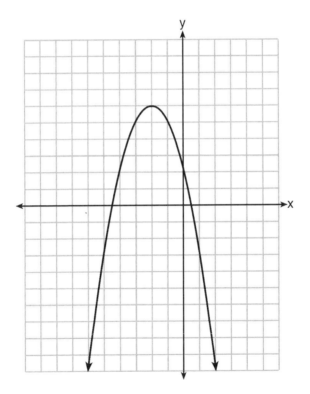

(1) (0,2) and $y = 2$ (3) (–2,6) and $y = -2$

(2) (0,2) and $x = 2$ (4) (–2,6) and $x = -2$

18. The graph of a parabola is represented by the equation $y = ax^2$ where a is a positive integer. If a is multiplied by 2, the new parabola will become

(1) narrower and open downward

(2) narrower and open upward

(3) wider and open downward

(4) wider and open upward

June 2012 – 14, 34

14. What is the vertex of the parabola represented by the equation $y = -2x^2 + 24x - 100$?

(1) $x = -6$ (3) $(6, -28)$

(2) $x = 6$ (4) $(-6, -316)$

34. On the set of axes below, graph the equation $y = x^2 + 2x - 8$. Using the graph, determine and state the roots of the equation $x^2 + 2x - 8 = 0$.

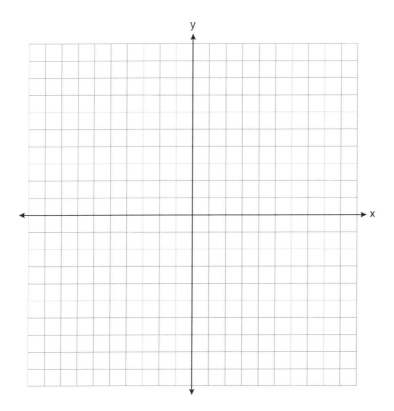

August 2011 – 11, 16, 18, 20

11.   What are the vertex and the axis of symmetry of the parabola shown in the graph below?

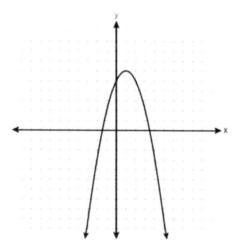

(1) vertex: $(1,6)$; axis of symmetry: $y = 1$
(2) vertex: $(1,6)$; axis of symmetry: $x = 1$
(3) vertex: $(6,1)$; axis of symmetry: $y = 1$
(4) vertex: $(6,1)$; axis of symmetry: $x = 1$

16.   The length of a rectangle is 3 inches more than its width. The area of the rectangle is 40 square inches. What is the length, in inches, of the rectangle?

(1) 5   (3) 8.5

(2) 8   (4) 11.

18. Which equation represents a quadratic function?

    (1) $y = x + 2$ (3) $y = x^2$

    (2) $y = |x + 2|$ (4) $y = 2^x$

20. What are the roots of the equation $x^2 - 5x + 6 = 0$?

    (1) 1 and -6 (3) -1 and 6

    (2) 2 and 3   (4) -2 and -3

June 2011 – 13, 33

13. Melissa graphed the equation $y = x^2$ and Dave graphed the equation $y = -3x^2$ on the same coordinate grid. What is the relationship between the graphs that Melissa and Dave drew?

    (1)   Dave's graph is wider and opens in the opposite direction from Melissa's graph.

    (2)   Dave's graph is narrower and opens in the opposite direction from Melissa's graph.

    (3)   Dave's graph is wider and is three units below Melissa's graph.

    (4)   Dave's graph is narrower and is three units to the left of Melissa's graph.

33. State the equation of the axis of symmetry and the coordinates of the vertex of the parabola graphed below.

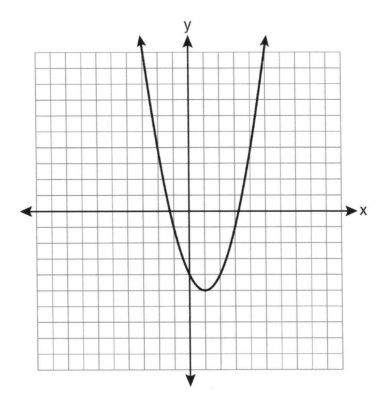

August 2010 – 15, 18, 36

15. The diagram below shows the graph of $y = -x^2 - c$.

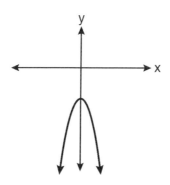

Which diagram shows the graph of $y = x^2 - c$?

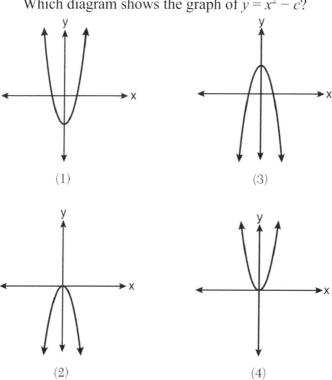

(1)

(3)

(2)

(4)

18. The height, y, of a ball tossed into the air can be represented by the equation $y = -x^2 + 10x + 3$, where x is the elapsed time. What is the equation of the axis of symmetry of this parabola?

(1) $y = 5$ (3) $x = 5$

(2) $y = -5$ (4) $x = -5$

36. Find the roots of the equation $x^2 = 30 - 13x$ algebraically.

June 2010 – 5, 20

5. What are the vertex and axis of symmetry of the parabola shown in the diagram below?

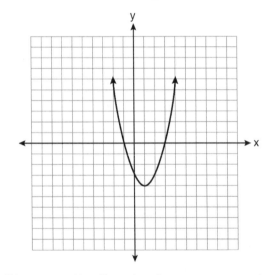

(1) vertex: $(1,-4)$; axis of symmetry: $x = 1$
(2) vertex: $(1,-4)$; axis of symmetry: $x = -4$
(3) vertex: $(-4,1)$; axis of symmetry: $x = 1$
(4) vertex: $(-4,1)$; axis of symmetry: $x = -4$

20. When 36 is subtracted from the square of a number, the result is five times the number. What is the positive solution?

(1) 9   (3) 3

(2) 6   (4) 4

August 2009 – 16, 21, 34

16. The equation $y = -x^2 - 2x + 8$ is graphed on the set of axes below.

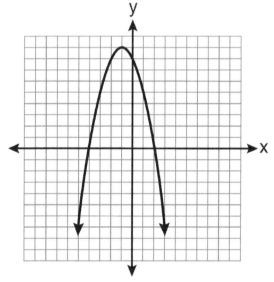

Based on this graph, what are the roots of the equation $-x^2 - 2x + 8 = 0$?

(1) 8 and 0   (3) 9 and −1

(2) 2 and −4   (4) 4 and −2

21. The solution to the equation $x^2 - 6x = 0$ is

(1) 0, only   (3) 0 and 6

(2) 6, only   (4) $\pm\sqrt{6}$

34. Find algebraically the equation of the axis of symmetry and the coordinates of the vertex of the parabola whose equation is $y = -2x^2 - 8x + 3$.

June 2009 – 2, 18, 24

2. What are the roots of the equation $x^2 - 7x + 6 = 0$?

(1) 1 and 7   (3) −1 and −6

(2) −1 and 7   (4) 1 and 6

18. What are the vertex and axis of symmetry of the parabola $y = x^2 - 16x + 63$?

(1) vertex: (8,−1); axis of symmetry: $x = 8$
(2) vertex: (8,1); axis of symmetry: $x = 8$
(3) vertex: (−8,−1); axis of symmetry: $x = -8$
(4) vertex: (−8,1); axis of symmetry: $x = -8$

24. The equation $y = x^2 + 3x - 18$ is graphed on the set of axes below.

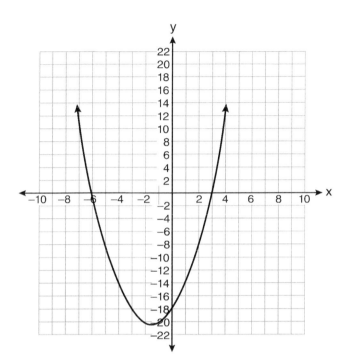

Based on this graph, what are the roots of the equation $x^2 + 3x - 18 = 0$?

(1) −3 and 6   (3) 3 and −6

(2) 0 and −18   (4) 3 and −18

Linear-Quadratic Systems

August 2012 – 36

36. Solve the following system of equations algebraically for *all* values of *x* and *y*.

$$y = x^2 + 2x - 8$$
$$y = 2x + 1$$

June 2012 – 13

13. What is the solution set of the system of equations $x + y = 5$ and $y = x^2 - 25$?

(1) $\{(0, 5), (11, -6)\}$

(3) $\{(-5, 0), (6, 11)\}$

(2) $\{(5, 0), (-6, 11)\}$

(4) $\{(-5, 10), (6, -1)\}$

August 2011 – 38

38. On the set of axes below, solve the following system of equations graphically and state the coordinates of *all* points in the solution set.

$$y = -x^2 + 6x - 3$$
$$x + y = 7$$

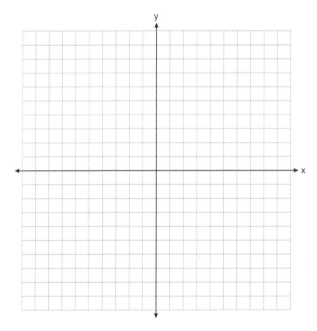

June 2011 – 18

18. Which ordered pair is a solution of the system of equations $y = x + 3$ and $y = x^2 - x$?

(1) (6,9)   (3) (3,−1)

(2) (3,6)   (4) (2,5)

August **2010 – 10**

10. Which graph can be used to find the solution of the
following system of equations?

$$y = x^2 + 2x + 3$$
$$2y - 2x = 10$$

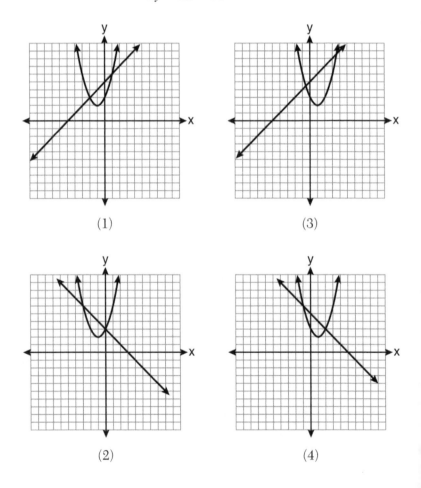

(1)

(3)

(2)

(4)

June 2010 – 39

39. On the set of axes below, solve the following system of equations graphically for all values of x and y.

$$y = -x^2 - 4x + 12$$
$$y = -2x + 4$$

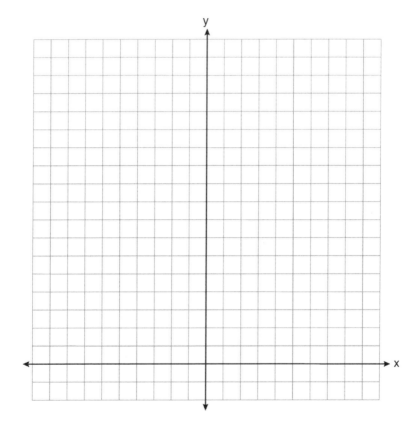

August 2009 - None

June 2009 – 39

39.   On the set of axes below, solve the following system
of equations graphically for all values of x and y.

$$y = x^2 - 6x + 1$$

$$y + 2x = 6$$

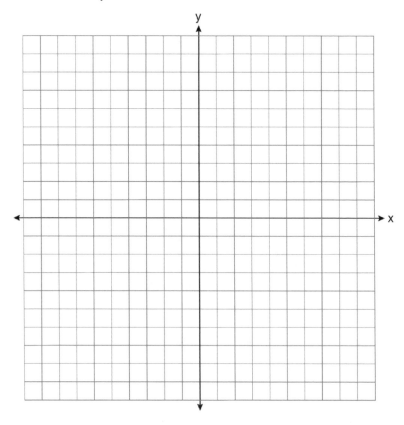

Perimeter; Circumference; Area of Common Figures

August 2012 – 28

28. What is the perimeter of the figure shown below, which consists of an isosceles trapezoid and a semicircle?

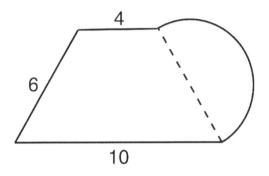

(1) $20 + 3\pi$ (3) $26 + 3\pi$

(2) $20 + 6\pi$ (4) $26 + 6\pi$

June 2012 – None

August 2011 – 28

28. A garden is in the shape of an isosceles trapezoid and a semicircle, as shown in the diagram below. A fence will be put around the perimeter of the entire garden.

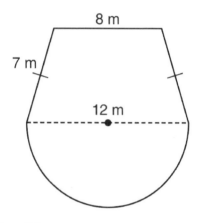

June 2011 – 31

31. The area of a rectangle is represented by $x^2 - 5x - 24$. If the width of the rectangle is represented by $x - 8$, express the length of the rectangle as a binomial.

August 2010 – 13, 19

13. What is the perimeter of a regular pentagon with a side whose length is $x + 4$?

(1) $x^2 + 16$ (3) $5x + 4$

(2) $4x + 16$ (4) $5x + 20$

19. In the diagram below, *MATH* is a rectangle, *GB* = 4.6, *MH* = 6, and *HT* = 15.

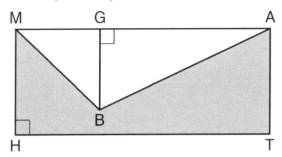

What is the area of polygon *MBATH*?

(1) 34.5   (3) 90.0

(2) 55.5   (4) 124.5

June 2010 – 29

29. A figure is made up of a rectangle and a semicircle as shown in the diagram below.

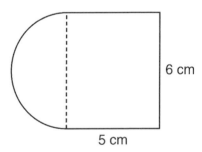

6 cm

5 cm

What is the area of the figure, to the *nearest tenth of a square centimeter*?

(1) 39.4   (3) 48.8

(2) 44.1   (4) 58.3

August 2009 – 24

24.   A playground in a local community consists of a
        rectangle and two semicircles, as shown in the
        diagram below.

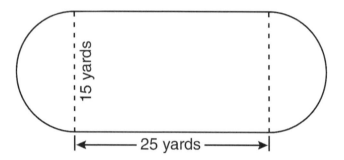

Which expression represents the amount of fencing,
in yards, that would be needed to completely enclose
the playground?

(1) $15\pi + 50$ (3) $30\pi + 50$

(2) $15\pi + 80$ (4) $30\pi + 80$

June 2009 – 34

34. In the diagram below, the circumference of circle O is 16π inches. The length of $\overline{BC}$ is three-quarters of the length of diameter $\overline{AD}$ and $CE = 4$ inches.

Calculate the area, in square inches, of trapezoid $ABCD$.

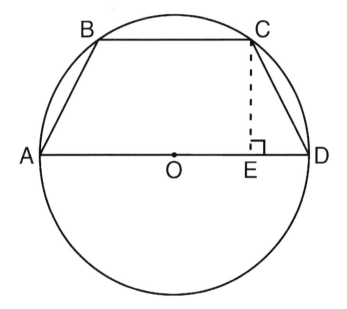

Volume and Surface Area; Relative Error in Measurement

August 2012 – 16, 24, 35

16. The rectangular prism shown below has a length of 3.0 cm, a width of 2.2 cm, and a height of 7.5 cm.

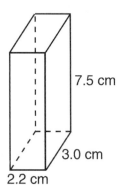

7.5 cm

3.0 cm

2.2 cm

What is the surface area, in square centimeters?

(1) 45.6   (3) 78.0

(2) 49.5   (4) 91.2

24. The volume of a cylindrical can is 32π cubic inches. If the height of the can is 2 inches, what is its radius, in inches?

(1) 8   (3) 16

(2) 2   (4) 4

35. Ashley measured the dimensions of a rectangular prism to be 6 cm by 10 cm by 1.5 cm. The actual dimensions are 5.9 cm by 10.3 cm by 1.7 cm. Determine the relative error, to the *nearest thousandth*, in calculating the volume of the prism.

June 2012 – 33, 37

33. Students calculated the area of a playing field to be 8,100 square feet. The actual area of the field is 7,678.5 square feet. Find the relative error in the area, to the *nearest thousandth.*

37. Mike buys his ice cream packed in a rectangular prism-shaped carton, while Carol buys hers in a cylindrical-shaped carton. The dimensions of the prism are 5 inches by 3.5 inches by 7 inches. The cylinder has a diameter of 5 inches and a height of 7 inches.

Which container holds more ice cream?

Justify your answer.

August 2011 – 5, 23

5. A cylinder has a diameter of 10 inches and a height of 2.3 inches. What is the volume of this cylinder, to the *nearest tenth of a cubic inch?*

(1) 72.3   (3) 180.6

(2) 83.1   (4) 722.6

23. Jack wants to replace the flooring in his rectangular kitchen. He calculates the area of the floor to be 12.8 square meters. The actual area of the floor is 13.5 square meters. What is the relative error in calculating the area of the floor, to the *nearest thousandth*?

(1) 0.051   (3) 0.054

(2) 0.052   (4) 0.055

June 2011 – 20, 36

20. The dimensions of a rectangle are measured to be 12.2 inches by 11.8 inches. The actual dimensions are 12.3 inches by 11.9 inches.

What is the relative error, to the *nearest ten-thousandth*, in calculating the area of the rectangle?

(1) 0.0168   (3) 0.0165

(2) 0.0167   (4) 0.0164

36. A plastic storage box in the shape of a rectangular prism has a length of $x + 3$, a width of $x - 4$, and a height of 5.

Represent the surface area of the box as a trinomial in terms of x.

August 2010 – 35

35. Find the volume, in cubic centimeters, *and* the surface area, in square centimeters, of the rectangular prism shown below.

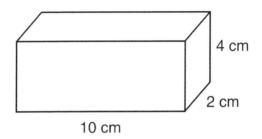

4 cm

2 cm

10 cm

June 2010 – 31

31. Alexis calculates the surface area of a gift box as 600 square inches. The actual surface area of the gift box is 592 square inches. Find the relative error of Alexis' calculation expressed as a decimal to the *nearest thousandth.*

August 2009 – 26, 32

26. Carrie bought new carpet for her living room. She calculated the area of the living room to be 174.2 square feet. The actual area was 149.6 square feet. What is the relative error of the area to the *nearest ten-thousandth?*

(1) 0.1412   (3) 1.8588

(2) 0.1644   (4) 2.1644

32.   The diagram below represents Joe's two fish tanks.

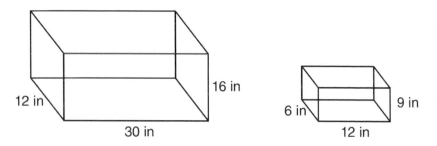

Joe's larger tank is completely filled with water.
He takes water from it to completely fill the small
tank. Determine how many cubic inches of water will
remain in the larger tank.

June 2009 – 28

28.   To calculate the volume of a small wooden cube,
Ezra measured an edge of the cube as 2 cm. The
actual length of the edge of Ezra's cube is 2.1 cm.

What is the relative error in his volume calculation
to the *nearest hundredth*?

(1) 0.13   (3) 0.15

(2) 0.14   (4) 0.16

Pythagorean Theorem

August 2012 – 38

38. In right triangle *ABC* shown below, *AC* = 29 inches, *AB* = 17 inches, and m ∠*ABC* = 90.

Find the number of degrees in the measure of angle *BAC*, to the *nearest degree*.

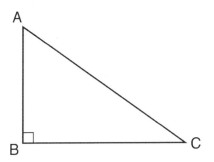

Find the length of $\overline{BC}$ to the *nearest inch*.

June 2012 – 23

23. The length of one side of a square is 13 feet. What is the length, to the *nearest foot,* of a diagonal of the square?

(1) 13   (3) 19

(2) 18   (4) 26

August 2011 – None

June 2011 – 2

2.   The legs of an isosceles right triangle each measure 10 inches. What is the length of the hypotenuse of this triangle, to the *nearest tenth of an inch*?

(1) 6.3   (3) 14.1

(2) 7.1   (4) 17.1

August 2010 – 4

4.   The end of a dog's leash is attached to the top of a 5-foot-tall fence post, as shown in the diagram below. The dog is 7 feet away from the base of the fence post.

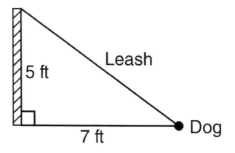

How long is the leash, to the *nearest tenth of a foot*?

(1) 4.9   (3) 9.0

(2) 8.6   (4) 12.0

June 2010 - None

August 2009 – 6

6.   Nancy's rectangular garden is represented in the diagram below.

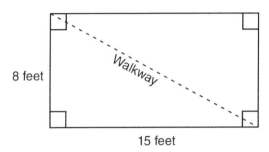

15 feet

If a diagonal walkway crosses her garden, what is its length, in feet?

(1) 17   (3) $\sqrt{161}$

(2) 22   (4) $\sqrt{529}$

June 2009 – 9

9.   What is the value of x, in inches, in the right triangle below?

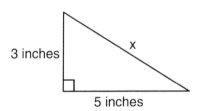

(1) $\sqrt{15}$ (3) $\sqrt{34}$

(2) 8   (4) 4

Right Triangle Trigonometry

August 2012 – 38

38. In right triangle *ABC* shown below, *AC* = 29 inches, *AB* = 17 inches, and m ∠*ABC* = 90. Find the number of degrees in the measure of angle *BAC*, to the *nearest degree*.

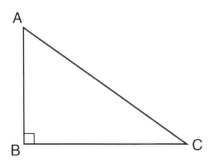

Find the length of $\overline{BC}$ to the *nearest inch*.

June 2012 – 24, 35

24. In △*ABC*, m∠*C* = 90. If *AB* = 5 and *AC* = 4, which statement is *not* true?

(1) $\cos A = \dfrac{4}{5}$

(2) $\tan A = \dfrac{3}{4}$

(3) $\sin B = \dfrac{4}{5}$

(4) $\tan B = \dfrac{5}{3}$

35. A 28-foot ladder is leaning against a house. The bottom of the ladder is 6 feet from the base of the house. Find the measure of the angle formed by the ladder and the ground, to the *nearest degree.*

August 2011 – 12, 26, 35

12. The diagram below shows right triangle *ABC*.

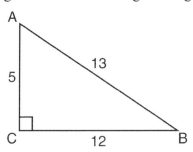

Which ratio represents the tangent of ∠*ABC?*

(1) $\dfrac{5}{13}$

(3) $\dfrac{12}{13}$

(2) $\dfrac{5}{12}$

(4) $\dfrac{12}{5}$

26. A right triangle contains a 38° angle whose adjacent side measures 10 centimeters. What is the length of the hypotenuse, to the nearest hundredth of a centimeter?

(1) 7.88

(3) 12.80

(2) 12.69

(4) 16.24

35.   A trapezoid is shown below.

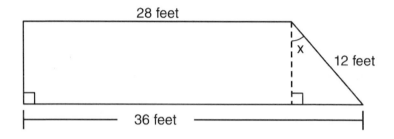

Calculate the measure of angle *x*, to the *nearest tenth of a degree.*

June 2011 – 8, 14

8.   An 8-foot rope is tied from the top of a pole to a stake in the ground, as shown in the diagram below.

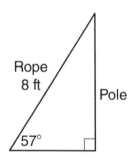

If the rope forms a 57° angle with the ground, what is the height of the pole, to the *nearest tenth of a foot?*

(1) 4.4   (3) 9.5

(2) 6.7   (4) 12.3

14. In right triangle *ABC* shown below, *AB* = 18.3 and *BC* = 11.2.

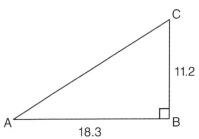

What is the measure of ∠*A*, to the *nearest tenth of a degree*?

(1) 31.5   (3) 52.3

(2) 37.7   (4) 58.5

August 2010 – 26, 39

26. Right triangle *ABC* has legs of 8 and 15 and a hypotenuse of 17, as shown in the diagram below.

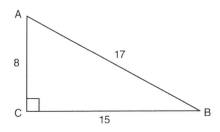

The value of the tangent of ∠*B* is

(1) 0.4706   (3) 0.8824

(2) 0.5333   (4) 1.8750

39.   A hot-air balloon is tied to the ground with two taut (straight) ropes, as shown in the diagram below. One rope is directly under the balloon and makes a right angle with the ground. The other rope forms an angle of 50° with the ground.

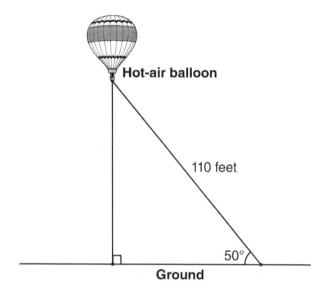

Determine the height, to the *nearest foot*, of the balloon directly above the ground.

Determine the distance, to the *nearest foot*, on the ground between the two ropes.

June 2010 – 9, 33

9. In $\triangle ABC$, the measure of $\angle B = 90°$, $AC = 50$, $AB = 48$, and $BC = 14$. Which ratio represents the tangent of $\angle A$?

(1) $\dfrac{14}{50}$

(3) $\dfrac{48}{50}$

(2) $\dfrac{14}{48}$

(4) $\dfrac{48}{14}$

33. A communications company is building a 30-foot antenna to carry cell phone   transmissions. As shown in the diagram below, a 50-foot wire from the top of the antenna to the ground is used to stabilize the antenna.

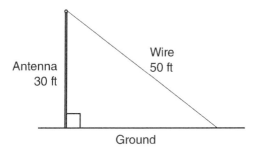

Find, to the *nearest degree*, the measure of the angle that the wire makes with the ground.

August 2009 – 14

14. A tree casts a 25-foot shadow on a sunny day, as shown in the diagram below.

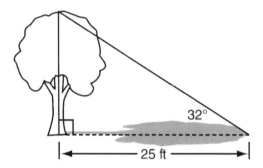

If the angle of elevation from the tip of the shadow to the top of the tree is 32°, what is the height of the tree to the *nearest tenth of a foot*?

(1) 13.2   (3) 21.2

(2) 15.6   (4) 40.0

June 2009 – 37

37.   A stake is to be driven into the ground away from the base of a 50-foot pole, as shown in the diagram below. A wire from the stake on the ground to the top of the pole is to be installed at an angle of elevation of 52°.

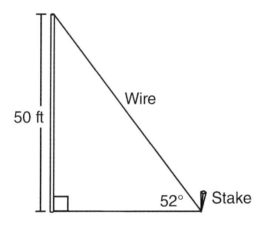

How far away from the base of the pole should the stake be driven in, to the *nearest foot*?

What will be the length of the wire from the stake to the top of the pole, to the *nearest foot*?

Probability

August 2012 – 29, 37

29. The probability that it will rain tomorrow is $\frac{1}{2}$. The probability that our team will win tomorrow's basketball game is $\frac{3}{5}$. Which expression represents the probability that it will rain and that our team will *not* win the game?

(1) $\frac{1}{2} + \frac{3}{5}$ (3) $\frac{1}{2} \times \frac{3}{5}$

(2) $\frac{1}{2} + \frac{2}{5}$ (4) $\frac{1}{2} \times \frac{2}{5}$

37. A company is running a contest and offering a first, second, and third prize. First prize is a Choice of a car or $15,000 cash. Second prize is a choice of a motorbike, a trip to New York City, or $2,000 cash. Third prize is a choice of a television or $500 cash.

If each prize is equally likely to be selected, list the sample space or draw a tree diagram of *all* possible different outcomes of first, second, and third prizes.

Determine the number of ways that *all* three prizes selected could be cash.

Determine the number of ways that *none* of the three prizes selected could be cash.

June 2012 – 18, 32

18. The bull's-eye of a dartboard has a radius of 2 inches and the entire board has a radius of 9 inches, as shown in the diagram below.

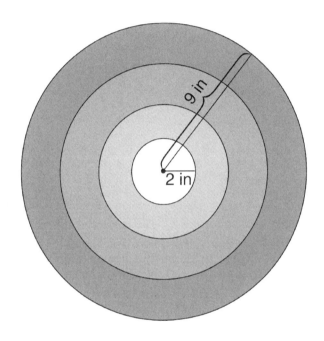

If a dart is thrown and hits the board, what is the probability that the dart will land in the bull's-eye?

(1) $\dfrac{2}{9}$ (3) $\dfrac{4}{81}$

(2) $\dfrac{7}{9}$ (4) $\dfrac{49}{81}$

32   Three storage bins contain colored blocks.
Bin 1 contains 15 red and 14 blue blocks.
Bin 2 contains 16 white and 15 blue blocks.
Bin 3 contains 15 red and 15 white blocks.
All of the blocks from the three bins are placed
into one box. If one block is randomly selected
from the box, which color block would most
likely be picked?

Justify your answer.

August 2011 – 25, 37

25.   Maria has a set of 10 index cards labeled with the
digits 0 through 9. She puts them in a bag and selects
one at random. The outcome that is most likely to
occur is selecting

(1) an odd number

(2) a prime number

(3) a number that is at most 5

(3) a number that is divisible by 3

37. Vince buys a box of candy that consists of Six chocolate pieces, four fruit-flavored pieces, and two mint pieces. He selects three pieces of candy at random, without replacement.

Calculate the probability that the first piece selected will be fruit flavored and the other two will be mint.

Calculate the probability that all three pieces selected will be the same type of candy.

June 2011 – 4, 38

4. The spinner shown in the diagram below is divided into six equal sections.

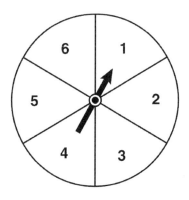

Which outcome is *least* likely to occur on a single spin?

(1) an odd number   (3) a perfect square

(2) a prime number   (4) a number divisible by 2

38. An outfit Jennifer wears to school consists of a top, a bottom, and shoes. Possible choices are listed below.

Tops:	T-shirt, blouse, sweater
Bottoms:	jeans, skirt, capris
Shoes:	flip-flops, sneakers

List the sample space or draw a tree diagram to represent all possible outfits consisting of one type of top, one type of bottom, and one pair of shoes.

Determine how many different outfits contain jeans and flip-flops.

Determine how many different outfits do *not* include a sweater.

August 2010 – 24, 38

24. The probability that it will snow on Sunday $\frac{3}{5}$. The probability that it will snow on both Sunday and Monday is $\frac{3}{10}$. What is the probability that it will snow on Monday, if it snowed on Sunday?

(1) $\dfrac{9}{50}$ (3) $\dfrac{1}{2}$

(2) 2 (4) $\dfrac{9}{10}$

38. Each of the hats shown below has colored marbles placed inside. Hat *A* contains five green marbles and four red marbles. Hat *B* contains six blue marbles and five red marbles. Hat *C* contains five green marbles and five blue marbles.

Hat A   Hat B   Hat C

If a student were to randomly pick one marble from each of these three hats, determine from which hat the student would most likely pick a green marble.

Justify your answer.

Determine the fewest number of marbles, if any, and the color of these marbles that could be added to *each* hat so that the probability of picking a green marble will be one-half in each of the three hats.

June 2010 – 6

6.   Three high school juniors, Reese, Matthew, and
     Chris, are running for student council president. A
     survey is taken a week before the election asking 40
     students which candidate they will vote for in the
     election.

     The results are shown in the table below.

Candidate's Name	Number of Students Supporting Candidate
Reese	15
Matthew	13
Chris	12

     Based on the table, what is the probability that a
     student will vote for Reese?

(1) $\dfrac{1}{3}$ (3) $\dfrac{3}{8}$

(2) $\dfrac{3}{5}$ (4) $\dfrac{5}{8}$

August 2009 – 7, 33

7. The spinner below is divided into eight equal regions and is spun once. What is the probability of *not* getting red?

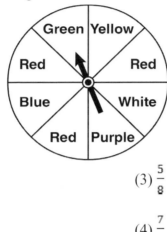

(1) $\dfrac{3}{5}$ (3) $\dfrac{5}{8}$

(2) $\dfrac{3}{8}$ (4) $\dfrac{7}{8}$

33. Clayton has three fair coins. Find the probability that he gets two tails and one head when he flips the three coins.

June 2009 – 8, 33

8.   Students in Ms. Nazzeer's mathematics class tossed a six-sided number cube whose faces are numbered 1 to 6. The results are recorded in the table below.

Result	Frequency
1	3
2	6
3	4
4	6
5	4
6	7

Based on these data, what is the empirical probability of tossing a 4?

(1) $\dfrac{8}{30}$ (3) $\dfrac{5}{30}$

(2) $\dfrac{6}{30}$ (4) $\dfrac{1}{30}$

33.   Some books are laid on a desk. Two are English, three are mathematics, one is French, and four are social studies. Theresa selects an English book and Isabelle then selects a social studies book. Both girls take their selections to the library to read. If Truman then selects a book at random, what is the probability that he selects an English book?

Permutations and Counting Methods

August 2012 – None

June 2012 – 39

39.   A large company must chose between two types
of passwords to log on to a computer. The first
type is a four-letter password using any of the 26
letters of the alphabet, without repetition of letters.
The second type is a six-digit password using the
digits 0 through 9, with repetition of digits allowed.

Determine the number of possible
four-letter passwords.

Determine the number of possible
six-digit passwords.

The company has 500,000 employees and needs a
different password for each employee.   State which
type of password the company should choose.

Explain your answer.

Aug 2011 - None

June 2011 - 9

9.   How many different ways can five books be arranged on a shelf ?

     (1) 5   (3) 25

     (2) 15   (4) 120

August 2010 – 28

28.   How many different four-letter arrangements are possible with the   letters G, A, R, D, E, N if each letter may be used only once?

     (1) 15   (3) 360

     (2) 24   (4) 720

June 2010 – 2, 26

2.   How many different sandwiches consisting of one type of cheese, one condiment, and one bread choice can be prepared from five types of cheese, two condiments, and three bread choices?

     (1) 10   (3) 15

     (2) 13   (4) 30

26. How many different three-letter arrangements can be formed using the letters in the word *ABSOLUTE* if each letter is used only once?

(1) 56   (3) 168

(2) 112   (4) 336

August 2009 – 5

5. The local ice cream stand offers three flavors of soft-serve ice cream: vanilla, chocolate, and strawberry; two types of cone: sugar and wafer; and three toppings: sprinkles, nuts, and cookie crumbs. If Dawn does not order vanilla ice cream, how many different choices can she make that have one flavor of ice cream, one type of cone, and one topping?

(1) 7   (3) 12

(2) 8   (4) 18

June 2009 – 31

31. Determine how many three-letter arrangements are possible with the letters *A, N, G, L,* and *E* if no letter may be repeated.

Statistics

August 2012 – 13, 34

13. Craig sees an advertisement for a car in a newspaper. Which information would *not* be classified as quantitative?

(1) the cost of the car

(2) the car's mileage

(3) the model of the car

(4) the weight of the car

34. The following cumulative frequency histogram shows the distances swimmers completed in a recent swim test.

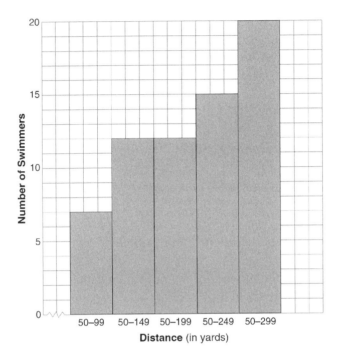

Based on the cumulative frequency histogram, determine the number of swimmers who swam between 200 and 249 yards.

Determine the number of swimmers who swam between 150 and 199 yards.

Determine the number of swimmers who took the swim test.

June 2012 – 2, 6, 7, 30

2. A survey is being conducted to determine if a cable company should add another sports channel to their schedule. Which random survey would be the *least* biased?

(1) surveying 30 men at a gym

(2) surveying 45 people at a mall

(4) surveying 50 fans at a football game

(4) surveying 20 members of a high school soccer team

6. Which situation is an example of bivariate data?

(1) the number of pizzas Tanya eats during her years in high school

(2) the number of times Ezra puts air in his bicycle tires during the summer

(3) the number of home runs Elias hits per game and the number of hours he practices baseball

(4) the number of hours Nellie studies for her mathematics tests during the first half of the school year

7. Brianna's score on a national math assessment exceeded the scores of 95,000 of the 125,000 students who took the assessment.
What was her percentile rank?

(1) 6   (3) 31

(2) 24   (4) 76

30. The cumulative frequency table below shows the length of time that 30 students spent text messaging on a weekend.

Minutes Used	Cumulative Frequency
31–40	2
31–50	5
31–60	10
31–70	19
31–80	30

Which 10-minute interval contains the first quartile?

(1) 31–40   (3) 51–60

(2) 41–50   (4) 61–70

August 2011 – 4, 6, 22, 32

4. Which situation does *not* describe a causal relationship?

(1) The higher the volume on a radio, the louder the sound will be.

(2) The faster a student types a research paper, the more pages the paper will have.

(3) The shorter the distance driven, the less gasoline that will be used.

(4) The slower the pace of a runner, the longer it will take the runner to finish the race.

6. Based on the box-and-whisker plot below, which statement is *false*?

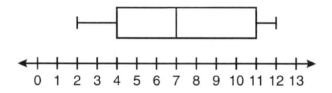

(1) The median is 7.
(2) The range is 12.
(3) The first quartile is 4.
(4) The third quartile is 11.

22. Which set of data can be classified as qualitative?

(1) scores of students in an algebra class

(2) ages of students in a biology class

(3) numbers of students in history classes

(4) eye colors of students in an economics class

32. Ms. Hopkins recorded her students' final exam scores in the frequency table below.

Interval	Tally	Frequency
61–70	︀卌	5
71–80	IIII	4
81–90	卌 IIII	9
91–100	卌 I	6

On the grid below, construct a frequency histogram based on the table.

June 2011 – 7, 34

7.   A survey is being conducted to determine which
      school board candidate would best serve the
      Yonkers community. Which group, when
      randomly surveyed, would likely produce the
      most bias?

      (1) 15 employees of the Yonkers school district

      (2) 25 people driving past Yonkers High School

      (3) 75 people who enter a Yonkers grocery store

      (4) 100 people who visit the local Yonkers
          shopping mall

34.   Given the following list of students' scores on a quiz:
      5, 12, 7, 15, 20, 14, 7

          Determine the median of these scores.

          Determine the mode of these scores.

      The teacher decides to adjust these scores by adding
      three points to each score.

      Explain the effect, if any, that this will have on the
      median and mode of these scores.

August 2010 – 17, 20, 34

17. Which phrase best describes the relationship between the number of miles driven and the amount of gasoline used?

  (1) causal, but not correlated
  (2) correlated, but not causal
  (3) both correlated and causal
  (4) neither correlated nor causal

20. This year, John played in 10 baseball games. In these games he had hit the ball 2, 3, 0, 1, 3, 2, 4, 0, 2, and 3 times. In the first 10 games he plays next year, John wants to increase his average (mean) hits per game by 0.5. What is the total number of hits John needs over the first10 games next year to achieve his goal?

  (1) 5   (3) 20

  (2) 2   (4) 25

34. The number of songs fifteen students have on their MP3 players is:

120, 124, 132, 145, 200, 255, 260, 292,

308, 314, 342, 407, 421, 435, 452

State the values of the minimum, 1st quartile, median, 3rd quartile, and maximum.

Using these values, construct a box-and-whisker plot using an appropriate scale on the line below.

June 2010 – 11, 17, 22, 38

11. Which table does *not* show bivariate data?

(1)

Height (inches)	Weight (pounds)
39	50
48	70
60	90

(2)

Gallons	Miles Driven
15	300
20	400
25	500

(3)

Quiz Average	Frequency
70	12
80	15
90	6

(4)

Speed (mph)	Distance (miles)
40	80
50	120
55	150

17. The freshman class held a canned food drive for 12 weeks. The results are summarized in the table below.

Canned Food Drive Results

Week	1	2	3	4	5	6	7	8	9	10	11	12
Number of Cans	20	35	32	45	58	46	28	23	31	79	65	62

Which number represents the second quartile of the number of cans of food collected?

(1) 29.5

(3) 40

(2) 30.5

(4) 60

22. Four hundred licensed drivers participated in the math club's survey on driving habits. The table below shows the number of drivers surveyed in each age group.

Ages of People in Survey on Driving Habits

Age Group	Number of Drivers
16–25	150
26–35	129
36–45	33
46–55	57
56–65	31

Which statement best describes a conclusion based on the data in the table?

(1) It may be biased because no one younger than 16 was surveyed.

(2) It would be fair because many different age groups were surveyed.

(3) It would be fair because the survey was conducted by the math club students.

(4) It may be biased because the majority of drivers surveyed were in the younger age intervals.

38.   The diagram below shows a cumulative
            frequency histogram of the students' test
            scores in Ms. Wedow's algebra class.

Ms. Wedow's Algebra Class Test Scores

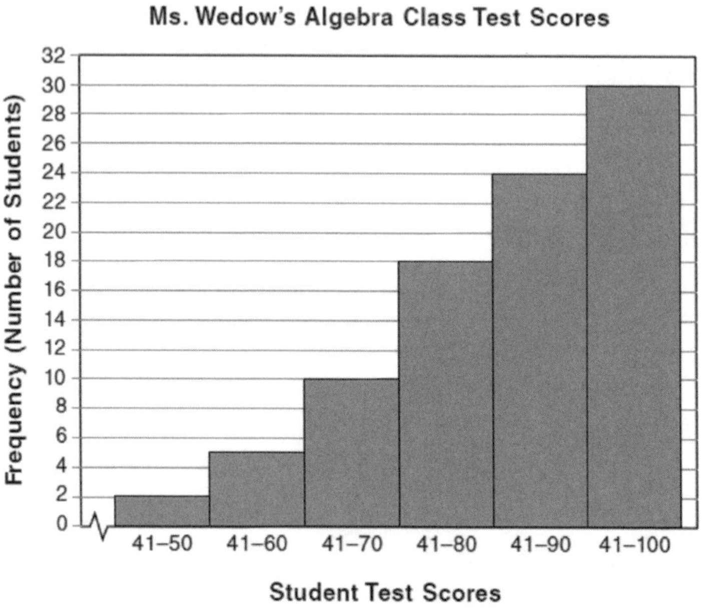

Determine the total number of students in the class.

Determine how many students scored higher than 70.

State which ten-point interval contains the median.

State which two ten-point intervals contain the same frequency.

August 2009 – 8, 10, 39

8. Which relationship can best be described as causal?

    (1) height and intelligence
    (2) shoe size and running speed
    (3) number of correct answers on a test and test score
    (4) number of students in a class and number of
        students with brown hair

10. Erica is conducting a survey about the proposed
    increase in the sports budget in the Hometown
    School District. Which survey method would likely
    contain the *most* bias?

    (1) Erica asks every third person entering the
        Hometown Grocery Store.

    (2) Erica asks every third person leaving the
        Hometown Shopping Mall this weekend.

    (3) Erica asks every fifth student entering
        Hometown High School on Monday morning.

    (4) Erica asks every fifth person leaving
        Saturday's Hometown High School football
        game.

39.   The test scores from Mrs. Gray's math class are shown below.

72, 73, 66, 71, 82, 85, 95, 85, 86, 89, 91, 92

Construct a box-and-whisker plot to display these data.

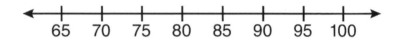

June 2009 – 5, 15, 38

5.   Which data set describes a situation that could be classified as qualitative?

(1) the ages of the students in Ms. Marshall's Spanish class

(2) the test scores of the students in Ms. Fitzgerald's class

(3) the favorite ice cream flavor of each of Mr. Hayden's students

(4) the heights of the players on the East High School basketball Team

15. The box-and-whisker plot below represents students' scores on a recent English test.

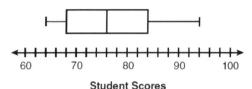

Student Scores

What is the value of the upper quartile?

(1) 68   (3) 84

(2) 76   (4) 94

38. The Fahrenheit temperature readings on 30 April mornings in Stormville, New York, are shown below.

41°, 58°, 61°, 54°, 49°, 46°, 52°, 58°, 67°, 43°,
47°, 60°, 52°, 58°, 48°, 44°, 59°, 66°, 62°, 55°,
44°, 49°, 62°, 61°, 59°, 54°, 57°, 58°, 63°, 60°

Using the data, complete the frequency table below.

Interval	Tally	Frequency
40–44		
45–49		
50–54		
55–59		
60–64		
65–69		

On the grid above, construct and label a Frequency histogram based on the table.

Arithmetic and Algebraic Applications

August 2012 – None

June 2012 – None

August 2011 – None

June 2011 - None

August 2010 - None

June 2010 - None

August 2009 – 28, 31, 35, 36

28.   The ages of three brothers are consecutive even
ntegers. Three times the age of the youngest brother
exceeds the oldest brother's age by 48 years.
What is the age of the *youngest* brother?

(1) 14   (3) 22

(2) 18   (4) 26

31. Chad complained to his friend that he had five equations to solve for homework. Are all of the homework problems equations?

Justify your answer.

Math Homework

1. $3x^2 \cdot 2x^4$

2. $5 - 2x = 3x$

3. $3(2x + 7)$

4. $7x^2 + 2x - 3x^2 - 9$

5. $\frac{2}{3} = \frac{x + 2}{6}$

Name _Chad_____

---

35. At the end of week one, a stock had increased in value from $5.75 a share to $7.50 a share. Find the percent of increase at the end of week one to the *nearest tenth of a percent*.

At the end of week two, the same stock had decreased in value from $7.50 to $5.75. Is the percent of decrease at the end of week two the same as the percent of increase at the end of week one?

Justify your answer.

36. The chart below compares two runners.

Runner	Distance, in miles	Time, in hours
Greg	11	2
Dave	16	3

Based on the information in this chart, state which runner has the faster rate.

Justify your answer.

June 2009 - None

The University of the State of New York

REGENTS HIGH SCHOOL EXAMINATION

INTEGRATED ALGEBRA

Wednesday, June 12, 2013 — 1:15 to 4:15 p.m., only

Student Name:_____

School Name: _____

Print your name and the name of your school on the lines above.

A separate answer sheet for Part I has been provided to you. Follow the instructions from the proctor for completing the student information on your answer sheet.

This examination has four parts, with a total of 39 questions. You must answer all questions in this examination. Record your answers to the Part I multiple-choice questions on the separate answer sheet. Write your answers to the questions in Parts II, III, and IV directly in this booklet. All work should be written in pen, except graphs and drawings, which should be done in pencil. Clearly indicate the necessary steps, including appropriate formula substitutions, diagrams, graphs, charts, etc. The formulas that you may need to answer some questions in this examination are found at the end of the examination. This sheet is perforated so you may remove it from this booklet.

Scrap paper is not permitted for any part of this examination, but you may use the blank spaces in this booklet as scrap paper. A perforated sheet of scrap graph paper is provided at the end of this booklet for any question for which graphing may be helpful but is not required. You may remove this sheet from this booklet. Any work done on this sheet of scrap graph paper will *not* be scored.

When you have completed the examination, you must sign the statement printed at the end of the answer sheet, indicating that you had no unlawful knowledge of the questions or answers prior to the examination and that you have neither given nor received assistance in answering any of the questions during the examination. Your answer sheet cannot be accepted if you fail to sign this declaration.

Notice…

A graphing calculator and a straightedge (ruler) must be available for you to use while taking this examination.

DO NOT OPEN THIS EXAMINATION BOOKLET UNTIL THE SIGNAL IS GIVEN.

Answer all 30 questions in this part. Each correct answer will receive 2 credits. Record your answers on your separate answer sheet. [60]

Use this space for computations.

1 Which expression represents "5 less than twice x"?

(1) $2x - 5$ (3) $2(5 - x)$

(2) $5 - 2x$ (4) $2(x - 5)$

2 Gabriella has 20 quarters, 15 dimes, 7 nickels, and 8 pennies in a jar. After taking 6 quarters out of the jar, what will be the probability of Gabriella randomly selecting a quarter from the coins left in the jar?

(1) $\dfrac{14}{44}$ (3) $\dfrac{14}{50}$

(2) $\dfrac{30}{44}$ (4) $\dfrac{20}{50}$

3 Based on the line of best fit drawn below, which value could be expected for the data in June 2015?

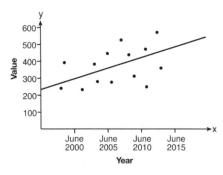

(1) 230   (3) 480

(2) 310   (4) 540

4 If the point $(5,k)$ lies on the line represented by the equation $2x + y = 9$, the value of k is

(1) 1   (3) −1

(2) 2   (4) −2

5 A soda container holds $5\frac{1}{2}$ gallons of soda. How many ounces of soda does this container hold?

> 1 quart = 32 ounces
> 1 gallon = 4 quarts

(1) 44   (3) 640

(2) 176   (4) 704

6 The roots of a quadratic equation can be found using the graph below.

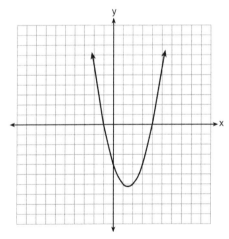

What are the roots of this equation?

(1) −4, only   (3) −1 and 4

(2) −4 and −1   (4) −4, −1, and 4

7 If the area of a rectangle is represented by $x^2 + 8x + 15$ and its length is represented by $x + 5$, which expression represents the width of the rectangle?

(1) $x + 3$ (3) $x^2 + 6x + 5$

(2) $x - 3$ (4) $x^2 + 7x + 10$

8 Which set of data describes a situation that would be classified as qualitative?

(1) the colors of the birds at the city zoo

(2) the shoe size of the zookeepers at the city zoo

(3) the heights of the giraffes at the city zoo

(4) the weights of the monkeys at the city zoo

9 The value of the expression $6! + \dfrac{5!(3!)}{4!} - 10$ is

(1) 50 (3) 740

(2) 102 (4) 750

10 Which interval notation represents $-3 \le x \le 3$?

(1) $[-3, 3]$ (3) $[-3, 3)$

(2) $(-3, 3]$ (4) $(-3, 3)$

11 The solutions of $x^2 = 16x - 28$ are

(1) -2 and -14 (3) -4 and -7

(2) 2 and 14 (4) 4 and 7

12 If the expression $(2y^a)^4$ is equivalent to $16y^8$, what is the value of a?

(1) 12　　　　　　　　　(3) 32

(2) 2　　　　　　　　　(4) 4

13 Which table shows bivariate data?

Age (yr)	Frequency
14	12
15	21
16	14
17	19
18	15

(1)

Time Spent Studying (hr)	Test Grade (%)
1	65
2	72
3	83
4	85
5	92

(3)

Type of Car	Average Gas Mileage (mpg)
van	25
SUV	23
luxury	26
compact	28
pickup	22

(2)

Day	Temperature (degrees F)
Monday	63
Tuesday	58
Wednesday	72
Thursday	74
Friday	78

(4)

14 The box-and-whisker plot below represents the results of test scores in a math class.

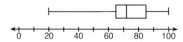

What do the scores 65, 85, and 100 represent?

(1) Q_1, median, Q_3

(2) Q_1, Q_3, maximum

(3) median, Q_1, maximum

(4) minimum, median, maximum

15 The expression $\dfrac{x-3}{x+2}$ is undefined when the value of x is

(1) −2, only   (3) 3, only

(2) −2 and 3   (4) −3 and 2

16 If $rx - st = r$, which expression represents x?

(1) $\dfrac{r+st}{r}$ (3) $\dfrac{r}{r-st}$

(2) $\dfrac{r}{r+st}$ (4) $\dfrac{r-st}{r}$

17 What is the solution of the equation $\dfrac{x+2}{2} = \dfrac{4}{x}$?

(1) 1 and −8

(2) 2 and −4

(3) −1 and 8

(4) −2 and 4

18 Which type of function is graphed below?

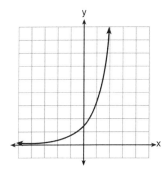

(1) linear   (3) exponential

(2) quadratic   (4) absolute value

19 What is the slope of the line represented by the equation $4x + 3y = 12$?

(1) $\dfrac{4}{3}$ (3) $-\dfrac{3}{4}$

(2) $\dfrac{3}{4}$ (4) $-\dfrac{4}{3}$

20 The diagram below shows the graph of which inequality?

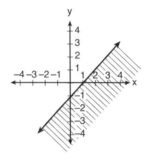

(1) $y > x - 1$ (3) $y < x - 1$

(2) $y \geq x - 1$ (4) $y \leq x - 1$

21 Carol plans to sell twice as many magazine subscriptions as Jennifer.
If Carol and Jennifer need to sell at least 90 subscriptions in all, which
inequality could be used to determine how many subscriptions, x,
Jennifer needs to sell?

(1) $x \geq 45$ (3) $2x - x \geq 90$

(2) $2x \geq 90$ (4) $2x + x \geq 90$

22 When $2x^2 - 3x + 2$ is subtracted from $4x^2 - 5x + 2$, the result is

(1) $2x^2 - 2x$ (3) $-2x^2 - 8x + 4$

(2) $-2x^2 + 2x$ (4) $2x^2 - 8x + 4$

23 Which expression represents the number of hours in w weeks and
d days?

(1) $7w + 12d$ (3) $168w + 24d$

(2) $84w + 24d$ (4) $168w + 60d$

24 Given:

$$R = \{1, 2, 3, 4\}$$
$$A = \{0, 2, 4, 6\}$$
$$P = \{1, 3, 5, 7\}$$

What is $R \cap P$?

(1) $\{0, 1, 2, 3, 4, 5, 6, 7\}$ (3) $\{1, 3\}$

(2) $\{1, 2, 3, 4, 5, 7\}$ (4) $\{2, 4\}$

25 Which equation could be used to find the measure of angle D in the right triangle shown in the diagram below?

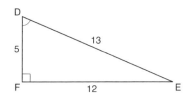

(1) $\cos D = \dfrac{12}{13}$ (3) $\sin D = \dfrac{5}{13}$

(2) $\cos D = \dfrac{13}{12}$ (4) $\sin D = \dfrac{12}{13}$

26 If the roots of a quadratic equation are -2 and 3, the equation can be written as

(1) $(x - 2)(x + 3) = 0$ (3) $(x + 2)(x + 3) = 0$

(2) $(x + 2)(x - 3) = 0$ (4) $(x - 2)(x - 3) = 0$

27 Which equation represents a line that is parallel to the y-axis and passes through the point (4,3)?

(1) $x = 3$ (3) $y = 3$

(2) $x = 4$ (4) $y = 4$

28 There are 18 students in a class. Each day, the teacher randomly selects three students to assist in a game: a leader, a recorder, and a timekeeper. In how many possible ways can the jobs be assigned?

(1) 306

(3) 4896

(2) 816

(4) 5832

29 In triangle RST, angle R is a right angle. If $TR = 6$ and $TS = 8$, what is the length of $\overline{RS}$?

(1) 10

(3) $2\sqrt{7}$

(2) 2

(4) $7\sqrt{2}$

30 How many solutions are there for the following system of equations?

$$y = x^2 - 5x + 3$$
$$y = x - 6$$

(1) 1

(3) 3

(2) 2

(4) 0

Answer all 3 questions in this part. Each correct answer will receive 2 credits. Clearly indicate the necessary steps, including appropriate formula substitutions, diagrams, graphs, charts, etc. For all questions in this part, a correct numerical answer with no work shown will receive only 1 credit. All answers should be written in pen, except for graphs and drawings, which should be done in pencil. [6]

31 Solve the inequality $-5(x - 7) < 15$ algebraically for x.

32 Oatmeal is packaged in a cylindrical container, as shown in the diagram below.

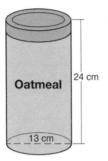

The diameter of the container is 13 centimeters and its height is 24 centimeters. Determine, in terms of π, the volume of the cylinder, in cubic centimeters.

33 The distance from Earth to Mars is 136,000,000 miles. A spaceship travels at 31,000 miles per hour. Determine, to the *nearest day*, how long it will take the spaceship to reach Mars.

159

Part III

Answer all 3 questions in this part. Each correct answer will receive 3 credits. Clearly indicate the necessary steps, including appropriate formula substitutions, diagrams, graphs, charts, etc. For all questions in this part, a correct numerical answer with no work shown will receive only 1 credit. All answers should be written in pen, except for graphs and drawings, which should be done in pencil. [9]

34 The menu for the high school cafeteria is shown below.

Main Course	Vegetable	Dessert	Beverage
veggie burger	corn	gelatin	milk
pizza	green beans	fruit salad	juice
tuna sandwich	carrots	yogurt	bottled water
frankfurter		cookie	
chicken tenders		ice cream cup	

Determine the number of possible meals consisting of a main course, a vegetable, a dessert, and a beverage that can be selected from the menu.

Determine how many of these meals will include chicken tenders.

If a student chooses pizza, corn or carrots, a dessert, and a beverage from the menu, determine the number of possible meals that can be selected.

35 A man standing on level ground is 1000 feet away from the base of a 350-foot-tall building. Find, to the *nearest degree*, the measure of the angle of elevation to the top of the building from the point on the ground where the man is standing.

36 Express $\sqrt{25} - 2\sqrt{3} + \sqrt{27} + 2\sqrt{9}$ in simplest radical form.

Part IV

Answer all 3 questions in this part. Each correct answer will receive 4 credits. Clearly indicate the necessary steps, including appropriate formula substitutions, diagrams, graphs, charts, etc. For all questions in this part, a correct numerical answer with no work shown will receive only 1 credit. All answers should be written in pen, except for graphs and drawings, which should be done in pencil. [12]

37 Solve algebraically: $\dfrac{2}{3x} + \dfrac{4}{x} = \dfrac{7}{x+1}$

[Only an algebraic solution can receive full credit.]

38 A jar contains five red marbles and three green marbles. A marble is drawn at random and not replaced. A second marble is then drawn from the jar.

Find the probability that the first marble is red and the second marble is green.

Find the probability that both marbles are red.

Find the probability that both marbles are the same color.

39 In the diagram below of rectangle *AFEB* and a semicircle with diameter $\overline{CD}$, *AB* = 5 inches, *AB* = *BC* = *DE* = *FE*, and *CD* = 6 inches. Find the area of the shaded region, to the *nearest hundredth of a square inch*.

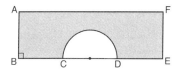

Scrap Graph Paper — This sheet will *not* be scored.

Tear Here

Tear Here

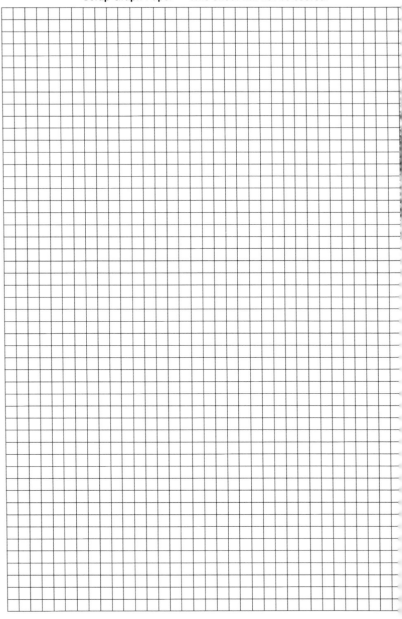

Reference Sheet

Trigonometric Ratios	$\sin A = \dfrac{opposite}{hypotenuse}$
	$\cos A = \dfrac{adjacent}{hypotenuse}$
	$\tan A = \dfrac{opposite}{adjacent}$

| Area | trapezoid $\quad A = \frac{1}{2}h(b_1 + b_2)$ |

| Volume | cylinder $\quad V = \pi r^2 h$ |

| Surface Area | rectangular prism $\quad SA = 2lw + 2hw + 2lh$ |
| | cylinder $\quad SA = 2\pi r^2 + 2\pi rh$ |

| Coordinate Geometry | $m = \dfrac{\Delta y}{\Delta x} = \dfrac{y_2 - y_1}{x_2 - x_1}$ |

The University of the State of New York

REGENTS HIGH SCHOOL EXAMINATION

INTEGRATED ALGEBRA

Tuesday, August 13, 2013 — 8:30 to 11:30 a.m., only

Student Name:_____

School Name: _____

The possession or use of any communications device is strictly prohibited when taking this examination. If you have or use any communications device, no matter how briefly, your examination will be invalidated and no score will be calculated for you.

Print your name and the name of your school on the lines above.

A separate answer sheet for Part I has been provided to you. Follow the instructions from the proctor for completing the student information on your answer sheet.

This examination has four parts, with a total of 39 questions. You must answer all questions in this examination. Record your answers to the Part I multiple-choice questions on the separate answer sheet. Write your answers to the questions in Parts II, III, and IV directly in this booklet. All work should be written in pen, except graphs and drawings, which should be done in pencil. Clearly indicate the necessary steps, including appropriate formula substitutions, diagrams, graphs, charts, etc. The formulas that you may need to answer some questions in this examination are found at the end of the examination. This sheet is perforated so you may remove it from this booklet.

Scrap paper is not permitted for any part of this examination, but you may use the blank spaces in this booklet as scrap paper. A perforated sheet of scrap graph paper is provided at the end of this booklet for any question for which graphing may be helpful but is not required. You may remove this sheet from this booklet. Any work done on this sheet of scrap graph paper will *not* be scored.

When you have completed the examination, you must sign the statement printed at the end of the answer sheet, indicating that you had no unlawful knowledge of the questions or answers prior to the examination and that you have neither given nor received assistance in answering any of the questions during the examination. Your answer sheet cannot be accepted if you fail to sign this declaration.

Notice…

A graphing calculator and a straightedge (ruler) must be available for you to use while taking this examination.

DO NOT OPEN THIS EXAMINATION BOOKLET UNTIL THE SIGNAL IS GIVEN.

168

Answer all 30 questions in this part. Each correct answer will receive 2 credits. No partial credit will be allowed. Record your answers on your separate answer sheet. [60]

Use this space for computations.

1 Which situation describes a negative correlation?

   (1) the amount of gas left in a car's tank and the amount of gas used from it

   (2) the number of gallons of gas purchased and the amount paid for the gas

   (3) the size of a car's gas tank and the number of gallons it holds

   (4) the number of miles driven and the amount of gas used

2 The sum of $8n^2 - 3n + 10$ and $-3n^2 - 6n - 7$ is

   (1) $5n^2 - 9n + 3$ (3) $-11n^2 - 9n - 17$

   (2) $5n^2 - 3n - 17$ (4) $-11n^2 - 3n + 3$

3 Which event is certain to happen?

   (1) Everyone walking into a room will have red hair.

   (2) All babies born in June will be males.

   (3) The Yankees baseball team will win the World Series.

   (4) The Sun will rise in the east.

4 Noj is 5 years older than Jacob. The product of their ages is 84. How old is Noj?

   (1) 6   (3) 12

   (2) 7   (4) 14

5 Marie currently has a collection of 58 stamps. If she buys s stamps each week for w weeks, which expression represents the total number of stamps she will have?

(1) $58sw$ (3) $58s + w$

(2) $58 + sw$ (4) $58 + s + w$

6 Given:

$A = \{$all odd integers from 1 through 19, inclusive$\}$

$B = \{9, 11, 13, 15, 17\}$

What is the complement of set B within set A?

(1) $\{3, 5, 7\}$ (3) $\{1, 3, 5, 7\}$

(2) $\{3, 5, 7, 19\}$ (4) $\{1, 3, 5, 7, 19\}$

7 Which equation represents a line that is parallel to the line whose equation is $y = -3x - 7$?

(1) $y = -3x + 4$ (3) $y = \frac{1}{3}x + 5$

(2) $y = -\frac{1}{3}x - 7$ (4) $y = 3x - 2$

8 Which graph does *not* represent the graph of a function?

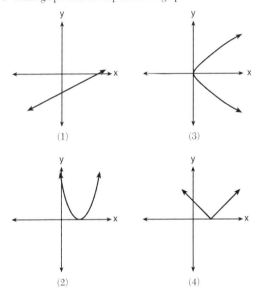

(1)   (3)

(2)   (4)

9 Which value of *x* is in the solution set of $-3x + 8 \geq 14$?

(1) -3 (3) 0

(2) -1 (4) 3

10 What is the slope of the line that passes through the points $(4, -7)$ and $(9, 1)$?

(1) $\frac{5}{8}$ (3) $-\frac{6}{12}$

(2) $\frac{8}{5}$ (4) $-\frac{13}{6}$

11 The product of $\frac{4x^2}{7y^2}$ and $\frac{21y^3}{20x^4}$, expressed in simplest form, is

(1) $0.6x^2y$

(3) $\frac{12x^2y^3}{20x^4y^2}$

(2) $\frac{3y}{5x^2}$

(4) $\frac{84x^2y^3}{140x^4y^2}$

12 The box-and-whisker plot below represents a set of grades in a college statistics class.

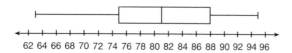

62 64 66 68 70 72 74 76 78 80 82 84 86 88 90 92 94 96

Which interval contains exactly 50% of the grades?

(1) 63–88   (3) 75–81

(2) 63–95   (4) 75–88

13 An art studio has a list of information posted with each sculpture that is for sale. Each entry in the list could be classified as quantitative *except* for the

(1) cost   (3) artist

(2) height   (4) weight

14 Which graph represents the inequality $y \geq x + 3$?

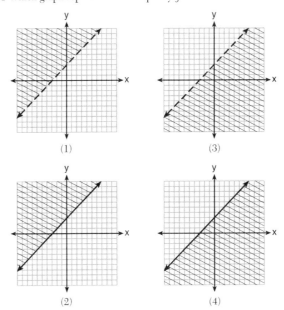

(1)

(2)

(3)

(4)

15 Using the substitution method, Ken solves the following system of equations algebraically.

$$2x - y = 5$$
$$3x + 2y = -3$$

Which equivalent equation could Ken use?

(1) $3x + 2(2x - 5) = -3$

(2) $3x + 2(5 - 2x) = -3$

(3) $3\left(y + \dfrac{5}{2}\right) + 2y = -3$

(4) $3\left(\dfrac{5}{2} - y\right) + 2y = -3$

16 A value of x that makes the expression $\dfrac{x^2 + 4x - 12}{x^2 - 2x - 15}$ undefined is

(1) -6 (3) 3

(2) -2 (4) 5

17 The statement $|-15| < x < |-20|$ is true when x is equal to

(1) -16 (3) 17

(2) -14 (4) 21

18 Which equation is true?

(1) $\dfrac{c^5}{d^7} \div \dfrac{d^3}{c} = \dfrac{c^4}{d^4}$ (3) $\left(\dfrac{s^3 t^8}{s^4 t^5}\right)^2 = \dfrac{t^5}{s^2}$

(2) $(-2m^2 p)^3 = -8m^6 p^3$ (4) $(-2a^2 b^3)(3ab^2) = a^3 b^5$

19 The equation $3(4x) = (4x)3$ illustrates which property?

(1) commutative   (3) distributive

(2) associative   (4) multiplicative inverse

20 Monique has three sons who play football, two sons who play baseball, and one son who plays both sports. If all of her sons play baseball or football, how many sons does she have?

(1) 5   (3) 3

(2) 6   (4) 4

21 Written in set-builder notation, $S = \{1, 3, 5, 7, 9\}$ is

   (1) $\{x|1 < x < 9$, where x is a prime number$\}$

   (2) $\{x|1 \leq x \leq 9$, where x is a prime number$\}$

   (3) $\{x|1 < x < 9$, where x is an odd integer$\}$

   (4) $\{x|1 \leq x \leq 9$, where x is an odd integer$\}$

22 Which is the equation of a parabola that has the same vertex as the parabola represented by $y = x^2$, but is wider?

   (1) $y = x^2 + 2$ (3) $y = 2x^2$

   (2) $y = x^2 - 2$ (4) $y = \frac{1}{2}x^2$

23 In right triangle ABC, $m\angle C = 90$, $AC = 7$, and $AB = 13$. What is the length of $\overline{BC}$?

   (1) 6   (3) $\sqrt{120}$

   (2) 20   (4) $\sqrt{218}$

24 A cube, with faces numbered 1 to 6, is rolled, and a penny is tossed at the same time. How many elements in the sample space consist of an even number and a tail?

   (1) 12   (3) 3

   (2) 2   (4) 4

25 If the volume of a cube is 8 cubic centimeters, what is its surface area, in square centimeters?

   (1) 32   (3) 12

   (2) 24   (4) 4

26 A designer created a garden, as shown in the diagram below. The garden consists of four quarter-circles of equal size inside a square. The designer put a fence around both the inside and the outside of the garden.

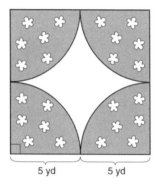

5 yd   5 yd

Which expression represents the amount of fencing, in yards, that the designer used for the fence?

(1) $40 + 10\pi$ (3) $100 + 10\pi$

(2) $40 + 25\pi$ (4) $100 + 25\pi$

27 Mr. Taylor raised all his students' scores on a recent test by five points. How were the mean and the range of the scores affected?

(1) The mean increased by five and the range increased by five.

(2) The mean increased by five and the range remained the same.

(3) The mean remained the same and the range increased by five.

(4) The mean remained the same and the range remained the same.

28 Which fraction is equivalent to $\dfrac{4}{3a} - \dfrac{5}{2a}$?

(1) $-\dfrac{1}{a}$ (3) $-\dfrac{7}{6a}$

(2) $-\dfrac{1}{5a}$ (4) $-\dfrac{7}{6a^2}$

29 Which ratio represents the cosine of angle A in the right triangle below?

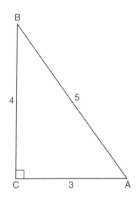

(1) $\frac{3}{5}$ (3) $\frac{4}{5}$

(2) $\frac{5}{3}$ (4) $\frac{4}{3}$

30 If $2y + 2w = x$, then w, in terms of x and y, is equal to

(1) $x - y$ (3) $x + y$

(2) $\frac{x - 2y}{2}$ (4) $\frac{x + 2y}{2}$

Part II

Answer all 3 questions in this part. Each correct answer will receive 2 credits. Clearly indicate the necessary steps, including appropriate formula substitutions, diagrams, graphs, charts, etc. For all questions in this part, a correct numerical answer with no work shown will receive only 1 credit. All answers should be written in pen, except for graphs and drawings which should be done in pencil. [6]

31 A jogger ran at a rate of 5.4 miles per hour. Find the jogger's *exact* rate, in feet per minute.

1 mile = 5,280 feet

32 Express $2\sqrt{108}$ in simplest radical form.

179

33 Adrianne invested $2000 in an account at a 3.5% interest rate compounded annually. She made no deposits or withdrawals on the account for 4 years. Determine, to the *nearest dollar*, the balance in the account after the 4 years.

Answer all 3 questions in this part. Each correct answer will receive 3 credits. Clearly indicate the necessary steps, including appropriate formula substitutions, diagrams, graphs, charts, etc. For all questions in this part, a correct numerical answer with no work shown will receive only 1 credit. All answers should be written in pen, except for graphs and drawings, which should be done in pencil. [9]

34 Miller's Department Store is having a sale with a 25% discount on mattresses. If the sales tax rate is 8%, how much change will Frank receive from $800 if he purchases a mattress regularly priced at $895 during this sale?

35 The difference between two numbers is 28. The larger number is 8 less than twice the smaller number. Find *both* numbers.

[Only an algebraic solution can receive full credit.]

36 Janis measures the dimensions of the floor in her rectangular classroom for a rug. Her measurements are 10.50 feet by 12.25 feet. The actual measurements of the floor are 10.75 feet by 12.50 feet. Determine the relative error in calculating the area, to the *nearest thousandth*.

Answer all 3 questions in this part. Each correct answer will receive 4 credits. Clearly indicate the necessary steps, including appropriate formula substitutions, diagrams, graphs, charts, etc. For all questions in this part, a correct numerical answer with no work shown will receive only 1 credit. All answers should be written in pen, except for graphs and drawings, which should be done in pencil. [12]

37 On the set of axes below, graph the following system of equations. Using the graph, determine and state *all* solutions of the system of equations.

$$y = -x^2 - 2x + 3$$
$$y + 1 = -2x$$

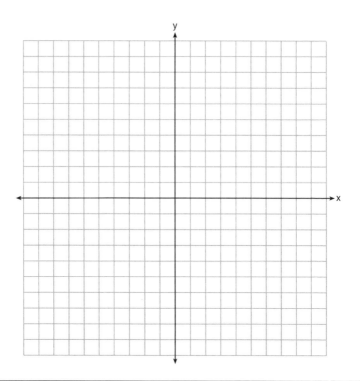

38 Express $\dfrac{3x^2 + 9x}{x^2 + 5x + 6} \div \dfrac{x^2 - 9}{x^2 - x - 6}$ in simplest form.

[18]

39 A bottle contains 12 red marbles and 8 blue marbles. A marble is chosen at random and not replaced. Then, a second marble is chosen at random.

Determine the probability that the two marbles are *not* the same color.

Determine the probability that *at least* one of the marbles is red.

Reference Sheet

Trigonometric Ratios

$$\sin A = \frac{opposite}{hypotenuse}$$

$$\cos A = \frac{adjacent}{hypotenuse}$$

$$\tan A = \frac{opposite}{adjacent}$$

Area

trapezoid $\quad A = \frac{1}{2}h(b_1 + b_2)$

Volume

cylinder $\quad V = \pi r^2 h$

Surface Area

rectangular prism $\quad SA = 2lw + 2hw + 2lh$

cylinder $\quad SA = 2\pi r^2 + 2\pi rh$

Coordinate Geometry

$$m = \frac{\Delta y}{\Delta x} = \frac{y_2 - y_1}{x_2 - x_1}$$

June 19, 2009 – 1:15 to 4:15 p.m.

Part I
Allow a total of 60 credits, 2 credits for each of the following. Allow credit if the student has written the correct answer instead of the numeral 1, 2, 3, or 4.

(1) 4	(9) 3	(17) 1	(25) 2
(2) 4	(10) 2	(18) 1	(26) 3
(3) 1	(11) 4	(19) 3	(27) 4
(4) 2	(12) 2	(20) 1	(28) 2
(5) 3	(13) 3	(21) 2	(29) 2
(6) 4	(14) 1	(22) 1	(30) 4
(7) 1	(15) 3	(23) 2	
(8) 2	(16) 4	(24) 3	

Part II

For each question, use the specific criteria to award a maximum of two credits. Unless otherwise specified, mathematically correct alternative solutions should be awarded appropriate credit.

(31) **[2]** 60, and appropriate work is shown, such as $_5P_3$ or $5 \times 4 \times 3$.

(32) **[2]** $4x(x - 3)(x + 3)$, and appropriate work is shown.

(33) **[2]** 1/8 or an equivalent answer, and appropriate work is shown.

Part III

For each question, use the specific criteria to award a maximum of three credits. Unless otherwise specified, mathematically correct alternative solutions should be awarded appropriate credit.

(34) **[3]** 56, and appropriate work is shown.

(35) **[3]** 5,583.86, and appropriate work is shown.

(36) **[3]** The data are plotted correctly **(1, 30), (2, 35), (5, 55), (7, 60), (10, 70)** an appropriate line of best fit is drawn, and its equation **$y = 5x + 25$** is stated

Part IV
For each question, use the specific criteria to award a
maximum of four credits. Unless otherwise specified,
mathematically correct alternative solutions should be
awarded appropriate credit.

(37) **[4]** 39 and 63, and appropriate work is shown,
such as using trigonometry or the Pythagorean
theorem.

(38) **[4]** The frequency table is completed correctly,
and a correct frequency histogram is drawn
and labeled.

(39) **[4]** Both equations are graphed correctly,
and (–1,8) and (5,–4) are stated.

Map to Core Curriculum

Content Strand	Item Numbers
Number Sense and Operations	10, 26, 27, 31
Algebra	2, 3, 4, 6, 7, 9, 12, 13, 14, 16, 17, 18, 21, 22, 23, 25, 29, 30, 32, 35, 37
Geometry	19, 20, 24, 34, 39
Measurement	1, 11, 28
Probability and Statistics	5, 8, 15, 33, 36, 38

August 13, 2009 — 8:30 to 11:30 a.m.

Part I
Allow a total of 60 credits, 2 credits for each of the following. Allow credit if the student has written the correct answer instead of the numeral 1, 2, 3, or 4.

(1) 2	(9) 2	(17) 2	(25) 3
(2) 1	(10) 4	(18) 1	(26) 2
(3) 4	(11) 1	(19) 3	(27) 4
(4) 1	(12) 4	(20) 1	(28) 4
(5) 3	(13) 4	(21) 3	(29) 3
(6) 1	(14) 2	(22) 2	(30) 2
(7) 3	(15) 1	(23) 3	
(8) 3	(16) 2	(24) 1	

Part II

For each question, use the specific criteria to award a maximum of two credits. Unless otherwise specified, mathematically correct alternative solutions should be awarded appropriate credit.

(31) **[2]** "No," and an appropriate justification is given.

(32) **[2]** 5,112, and appropriate work is shown.

(33) **[2]** $\frac{3}{8}$ or an equivalent answer, and appropriate work is shown.

Part III

For each question, use the specific criteria to award a maximum of three credits. Unless otherwise specified, mathematically correct alternative solutions should be awarded appropriate credit.

(34) **[3]** $x = -2$ and $(-2, 11)$, and appropriate algebraic work is shown.

(35) **[3]** 30.4, and appropriate work is shown, and "no," and an appropriate justification is given.

(36) **[3]** Greg, and appropriate work is shown to justify the answer.

Part IV

For each question, use the specific criteria to award a maximum of four credits. Unless otherwise specified, mathematically correct alternative solutions should be awarded appropriate credit.

(37) **[4]** $\dfrac{x-7}{3x}$, and appropriate work is shown.

(38) **[4]** Both equations are graphed correctly, and at least one is labeled, and $(1,-3)$ is stated.

(39) **[4]** A box-and-whisker plot is constructed correctly, where the minimum = 66, the first quartile = 72.5, the median = 85, the third quartile = 90, and the maximum = 95.

Map to Learning Standards

Key Ideas	Item Numbers
Number Sense and Operations	22, 23, 35
Algebra	1, 2, 3, 4, 6, 9, 11, 12, 13, 14, 15, 17, 18, 20, 21, 27, 28, 29, 31, 34, 37
Geometry	16, 19, 24, 25, 32, 38
Measurement	26, 36
Statistics and Probability	5, 7, 8, 10, 30, 33, 39

June 18, 2010 — 1:15 to 4:15 p.m.

Part I
Allow a total of 60 credits, 2 credits for each of the following. Allow credit if the student has written the correct answer instead of the numeral 1, 2, 3, or 4.

(1) 4	(9) 2	(17) 3	(25) 4
(2) 4	(10) 1	(18) 4	(26) 4
(3) 3	(11) 3	(19) 3	(27) 2
(4) 2	(12) 3	(20) 1	(28) 4
(5) 1	(13) 4	(21) 1	(29) 2
(6) 3	(14) 3	(22) 4	(30) 1
(7) 3	(15) 2	(23) 2	
(8) 3	(16) 4	(24) 1	

Part II

For each question, use the specific criteria to award a maximum of two credits. Unless otherwise specified, mathematically correct alternative solutions should be awarded appropriate credit.

(31) **[2]** 0.014, and appropriate work is shown.

(32) **[2]** $-6a + 42$, and the distributive property is stated.

(33) **[2]** 37, and appropriate work is shown.

Part III

For each question, use the specific criteria to award a maximum of three credits. Unless otherwise specified, mathematically correct alternative solutions should be awarded appropriate credit.

(34) **[3]** -12, and appropriate work is shown, such as solving the inequality or substituting each value into the inequality and indicating its truth value.

(35) **[3]** Both equations are graphed correctly and at least one of the graphs is labeled, and an appropriate explanation is given, such as the graph becomes wider.

(36) **[3]** An appropriate line of best fit is drawn, and "No," and an appropriate justification is written.

Part IV
For each question, use the specific criteria to award a maximum of four credits. Unless otherwise specified, mathematically correct alternative solutions should be awarded appropriate credit.

(37) **[4]** $\dfrac{x+8}{3}$, and appropriate work is shown.

(38) **[4]** 30 students total are in the class, 20 students scored higher than 70, 71–80 is the interval containing the median, and 81–90 and 91–100 are the intervals containing the same frequency.

(39) **[4]** Both equations are graphed correctly, and (2,0) and (–4,12) are stated.

Map to Core Curriculum

Content Strands	Item Numbers
Number Sense and Operations	2, 8, 26, 32
Algebra	1, 3, 4, 7, 9, 10, 12, 14, 15, 16, 18, 19,20, 21, 23, 24, 27, 30, 33, 34, 37
Geometry	5, 13, 28, 29, 35, 39
Measurement	25, 31
Statistics and Probability	6, 11, 17, 22, 36, 38

August 18, 2010 – 8:30 to 11:30 a.m.

Part I
Allow a total of 60 credits, 2 credits for each of the following. Allow credit if the student has written the correct answer instead of the numeral 1, 2, 3, or 4.

(1) 3	(9) 3	(17) 3	(25) 4
(2) 1	(10) 1	(18) 3	(26) 2
(3) 2	(11) 4	(19) 2	(27) 3
(4) 2	(12) 2	(20) 4	(28) 3
(5) 2	(13) 4	(21) 2	(29) 2
(6) 4	(14) 2	(22) 4	(30) 1
(7) 2	(15) 1	(23) 2	
(8) 3	(16) 4	(24) 3	

Part II
For each question, use the specific criteria to award a maximum of two credits. Unless otherwise specified, mathematically correct alternative solutions should be awarded appropriate credit.

(31) **[2]** $3a^2b^2 - 6a$ or an equivalent simplified expression, and appropriate work is shown.

(32) **[2]** 2,160, and appropriate work is shown.

(33) **[2]** $-12\sqrt{3}$, and appropriate work is shown.

Part III
For each question, use the specific criteria to award a maximum of three credits. Unless otherwise specified, mathematically correct alternative solutions should be awarded appropriate credit.

(34) **[3]** Minimum = 120, first quartile = 145, median = 292, third quartile = 407, and maximum = 452 are indicated, and a correct box-and-whisker plot with an appropriate scale is drawn.

(35) **[3]** Volume = 80 and surface area = 136, and appropriate work is shown.

(36) **[3]** −15 and 2, and appropriate algebraic work is shown.

Part IV
For each question, use the specific criteria to award a maximum of four credits. Unless otherwise specified, mathematically correct alternative solutions should be awarded appropriate credit.

(37) **[4]** Both inequalities are graphed and shaded correctly, and at least one inequality is labeled, and the coordinates of a point in the solution set are stated.

(38) **[4]** Hat A and an appropriate justification is given, and 1 color that is not green in hat A, 11 green in hat B, and none in hat C, and appropriate work is shown.

(39) **[4]** 84 and 71, and appropriate work is shown.

Map to Core Curriculum

Content Strands	Item Numbers
Number Sense and Operations	6, 7, 28, 33
Algebra	2, 3, 4, 5, 8, 9, 11, 12, 13, 14, 16, 18, 21, 22, 26, 27, 29, 30, 31, 36, 39
Geometry	10, 15, 19, 25, 35, 37
Measurement	23, 32
Statistics and Probability	1, 17, 20, 24, 34, 38

June 16, 2011 – 1:15 to 4:15 p.m.

Part I
Allow a total of 60 credits, 2 credits for each of the
following. Allow credit if the student has written the correct
answer instead of the numeral 1, 2, 3, or 4.

1 . . . . . **3**	11 . . . . . **4**	21 . . . . . **2** . . . . .
2 . . . . . **3**	12 . . . . . **4**	22 . . . . . **2** . . . . .
3 . . . . . **1**	13 . . . . . **2**	23 . . . . . **4** . . . . .
4 . . . . . **3**	14 . . . . . **1**	24 . . . . . **2** . . . . .
5 . . . . . **2**	15 . . . . . **2**	25 . . . . . **4** . . . . .
6 . . . . . **3**	16 . . . . . **2**	26 . . . . . **1** . . . . .
7 . . . . . **1**	17 . . . . . **1**	27 . . . . . **2** . . . . .
8 . . . . . **2**	18 . . . . . **2**	28 . . . . . **2** . . . . .
9 . . . . . **4**	19 . . . . . **3**	29 . . . . . **4** . . . . .
10 . . . . .**3**	20 . . . . . **3**	30 . . . . . **4** . . . . .

Part II
For each question, use the specific criteria to award a maximum of 2 credits. Unless otherwise specified, mathematically correct alternative solutions should be awarded appropriate credit.

(31) **[2]** $x + 3$, and appropriate work is shown.

(32) **[2]** The distributive property in line 1 and commutative property in line 2 are identified.

(33) **[2]** $x = 1$ and $(1, -5)$ are stated.

Part III
For each question, use the specific criteria to award a maximum of 3 credits. Unless otherwise specified, mathematically correct alternative solutions should be awarded appropriate credit.

(34) **[3]** 12 and 7, and an appropriate explanation is given, such as both the median and mode will increase by 3.

(35) **[3]** A correct inequality is written and 15, and appropriate work is shown.

(36) **[3]** $2x^2 + 18x - 34$, and appropriate work is shown.

Part IV
For each question, use the specific criteria to award a maximum of 4 credits. Unless otherwise specified, mathematically correct alternative solutions should be awarded appropriate credit.

(37) **[4]** $-\dfrac{9}{4}$ or an equivalent answer, and appropriate algebraic work is shown.

(38) **[4]** A correct sample space or tree diagram is shown, And 3 and 12 are stated.

(39) **[4]** Both inequalities are graphed and shaded correctly, and at least one is labeled, and the coordinates of a point in the solution set are stated correctly.

Map to Core Curriculum

Content Strands	Item Numbers
Number Sense and Operations	6, 9, 27, 32
Algebra	1, 2, 3, 5, 8, 10, 12, 14, 18, 19, 21, 23, 24, 25, 26, 28, 29, 30, 31, 35, 37
Geometry	11, 13, 16, 33, 36, 39
Measurement	17, 20
Statistics and Probability	4, 7, 15, 22, 34, 38

August 17, 2011 — 8:30 to 11:30 a.m.,

Part I

Allow a total of 60 credits, 2 credits for each of the following. Allow credit if the student has written the correct answer instead of the numeral 1, 2, 3, or 4.

1 . . . . . 4	11 . . . . . 2	21 . . . . . 4 . . . . .
2 . . . . . 1	12 . . . . . 2	22 . . . . . 4 . . . . .
3 . . . . . 3	13 . . . . . 1	23 . . . . . 2 . . . . .
4 . . . . . 2	14 . . . . . 4	24 . . . . . 2 . . . . .
5 . . . . . 3	15 . . . . . 1	25 . . . . . 3 . . . . .
6 . . . . . 2	16 . . . . . 2	26 . . . . . 2 . . . . .
7 . . . . . 4	17 . . . . . 3	27 . . . . . 2 . . . . .
8 . . . . . 1	18 . . . . . 3	28 . . . . . 1 . . . . .
9 . . . . . 3	19 . . . . . 1	29 . . . . . 2 . . . . .
10 . . . . . 1	20 . . . . . 2	30 . . . . . 4 . . . . .

Part II
For each question, use the specific criteria to award a maximum of 2 credits. Unless otherwise specified, mathematically correct alternative solutions should be awarded appropriate credit.

(31) **[2]** $= \dfrac{ab}{b+a}$, and appropriate work is shown.

(32) **[2]** A correct frequency histogram is drawn and labeled.

(33) **[2]** 2.54, and appropriate work is shown.

Part III
For each question, use the specific criteria to award a maximum of 3 credits. Unless otherwise specified, mathematically correct alternative solutions should be awarded appropriate credit.

(34) **[3]** Both equations are graphed correctly, at least one is labeled, and an appropriate explanation is written.

(35) **[3]** 41.8, and appropriate work is shown.

(36) **[3]** $-2\sqrt{3}$, and appropriate work is shown.

Part IV

For each question, use the specific criteria to award a maximum of 4 credits. Unless otherwise specified, mathematically correct alternative solutions should be awarded appropriate credit.

(37) **[4]** $\dfrac{8}{1,320}$ and $\dfrac{144}{1,320}$ or equivalent answers, and appropriate work is shown.

(38) **[4]** Both equations are graphed correctly, and (2,5) and (5,2) are stated.

(39) **[4]** 15, and appropriate work is shown.

Map to Core Curriculum

Content Strands	Item Numbers
Number Sense and Operations	1, 13, 36
Algebra	3, 7, 8, 9, 10, 12, 14, 15, 16, 17, 19, 20, 21, 24, 26, 27, 29, 30, 31, 35, 39
Geometry	5, 11, 18, 28, 34, 38
Measurement	23, 33
Statistics and Probability	2, 4, 6, 22, 25, 32, 37

June 14, 2012 — 1:15 to 4:15 p.m.

Part I

Allow a total of 60 credits, 2 credits for each of the following. Allow credit if the student has written the correct answer instead of the numeral 1, 2, 3, or 4.

1 . . . . . 1	11 . . . . . 3	21 . . . . . 4 . . . . .
2 . . . . . 2	12 . . . . . 4	22 . . . . . 4 . . . . .
3 . . . . . 4	13 . . . . . 2	23 . . . . . 2 . . . . .
4 . . . . . 1	14 . . . . . 3	24 . . . . . 4 . . . . .
5 . . . . . 2	15 . . . . . 1	25 . . . . . 3 . . . . .
6 . . . . . 3	16 . . . . . 2	26 . . . . . 4 . . . . .
7 . . . . . 4	17 . . . . . 3	27 . . . . . 4 . . . . .
8 . . . . . 3	18 . . . . . 3	28 . . . . . 1 . . . . .
9 . . . . . 1	19 . . . . . 3	29 . . . . . 2 . . . . .
10 . . . . 3	20 . . . . . 1	30 . . . . . 3 . . . . .

Part II

For each question, use the specific criteria to award a maximum of 2 credits. Unless otherwise specified, mathematically correct alternative solutions should be awarded appropriate credit.

(31) **[2]** 2, and appropriate algebraic work is shown.

(32) **[2]** White, and an appropriate justification is given.

(33) **[2]** 0.055, and appropriate work is shown.

Part III

For each question, use the specific criteria to award a maximum of 3 credits. Unless otherwise specified, mathematically correct alternative solutions should be awarded appropriate credit.

(34) **[3]** The equation is graphed correctly, and – 4 and 2 are stated.

(35) **[3]** 78, and appropriate work is shown.

(36) **[3]** 6 3, and appropriate work is shown.

Part IV
For each question, use the specific criteria to award a maximum of 4 credits. Unless otherwise specified, mathematically correct alternative solutions should be awarded appropriate credit.

(37) **[4]** Cylinder or Carol's, and an appropriate justification is given, and 14.9, and appropriate work is shown.

(38) **[4]** 4, and appropriate algebraic work is shown.

(39) **[4]** 358,800 and 1,000,000, and six-digit or numeric password, and appropriate work is shown, and an appropriate explanation is written.

Map to Core Curriculum

Content Strands	Item Numbers
Number Sense and Operations	36, 39
Algebra	3, 4, 8, 10, 11, 13, 14, 15, 16, 17, 19, 20, 22, 23, 24, 25, 26, 27, 29, 31, 35, 38
Geometry	9, 12, 21, 34, 37
Measurement	1, 28, 33
Statistics and Probability	2, 5, 6, 7, 18, 30, 32

August 16, 2012 — 8:30 to 11:30 a.m.

Part I
Allow a total of 60 credits, 2 credits for each of the following.

1 . . . . . 3	11 . . . . . 3	21 . . . . . 3 . . . . .
2 . . . . . 3	12 . . . . . 2	22 . . . . . 4 . . . . .
3 . . . . . 3	13 . . . . . 3	23 . . . . . 2 . . . . .
4 . . . . . 1	14 . . . . . 4	24 . . . . . 4 . . . . .
5 . . . . . 2	15 . . . . . 2	25 . . . . . 3 . . . . .
6 . . . . . 4	16 . . . . . 4	26 . . . . . 3 . . . . .
7 . . . . . 3	17 . . . . . 4	27 . . . . . 2 . . . . .
8 . . . . . 3	18 . . . . . 2	28 . . . . . 1 . . . . .
9 . . . . . 1	19 . . . . . 3	29 . . . . . 4 . . . . .
10 . . . . 4	20 . . . . . 1	30 . . . . . 3 . . . . .

Part II

For each question, use the specific criteria to award a maximum of 2 credits. Unless otherwise specified, mathematically correct alternative solutions should be awarded appropriate credit.

(31) **[2]** 6.56×10^{-2}

(32) **[2]** $\dfrac{2(x+5)}{x+4}$ and $\dfrac{2x+10}{x+4}$, and appropriate work is shown.

(33) **[2]** A correct graph is drawn over the given interval.

Part III

For each question, use the specific criteria to award a maximum of 3 credits. Unless otherwise specified, mathematically correct alternative solutions should be awarded appropriate credit.

(34) **[3]** All three answers (3, 0, and 20) are correct.

(35) **[3]** 0.129, and appropriate work is shown.

(36) **[3]** $x = -3$, $y = -5$ and $x = 3$, $y = 7$ or $(-3, -5)$ and $(3, 7)$, and appropriate algebraic work is shown.

Part IV
For each question, use the specific criteria to award a maximum of 4 credits. Unless otherwise specified, mathematically correct alternative solutions should be awarded appropriate credit.

(37) **[4]** A correct tree diagram or sample space is shown, and 1 and 2 are stated.

(38) **[4]** 54 and 23, and appropriate work is shown.

(39) **[4]** Both inequalities are graphed and shaded correctly, and at least one is labeled, and the coordinates of a point that satisfies $y + x \geq 3$, but not $5x - 2y > 10$ are stated.

Map to Core Curriculum

Content Strands	Item Numbers
Number Sense and Operations	9, 20, 31
Algebra	3, 5, 6, 7, 11, 12, 15, 17, 19, 21, 22, 23, 25, 26, 27, 30, 32, 36, 38
Geometry	1, 14, 16, 18, 24, 28, 33, 39
Measurement	2, 10, 35
Statistics and Probability	4, 8, 13, 29, 34, 37

June 14, 2012 — 1:15 to 4:15 p.m.

Part I

Allow a total of 60 credits, 2 credits for each of the following. Allow credit if the student has written the correct answer instead of the numeral 1, 2, 3, or 4.

1 . . . . . 1	11 . . . . . 3	21 . . . . . 4 . . . . .
2 . . . . . 2	12 . . . . . 4	22 . . . . . 4 . . . . .
3 . . . . . 4	13 . . . . . 2	23 . . . . . 2 . . . . .
4 . . . . . 1	14 . . . . . 3	24 . . . . . 4 . . . . .
5 . . . . . 2	15 . . . . . 1	25 . . . . . 3 . . . . .
6 . . . . . 3	16 . . . . . 2	26 . . . . . 4 . . . . .
7 . . . . . 4	17 . . . . . 3	27 . . . . . 4 . . . . .
8 . . . . . 3	18 . . . . . 3	28 . . . . . 1 . . . . .
9 . . . . . 1	19 . . . . . 3	29 . . . . . 2 . . . . .
10 . . . . 3	20 . . . . . 1	30 . . . . . 3 . . . . .

Part II
For each question, use the specific criteria to award a maximum of 2 credits. Unless otherwise specified, mathematically correct alternative solutions should be awarded appropriate credit.

(31) **[2]** 2, and appropriate algebraic work is shown.

(32) **[2]** White, and an appropriate justification is given.

(33) **[2]** 0.055, and appropriate work is shown.

Part III
For each question, use the specific criteria to award a maximum of 3 credits. Unless otherwise specified, mathematically correct alternative solutions should be awarded appropriate credit.

(34) **[3]** The equation is graphed correctly,
        and – 4 and 2 are stated.

(35) **[3]** 78, and appropriate work is shown.

(36) **[3]** 6 3, and appropriate work is shown.

Part IV
For each question, use the specific criteria to award a maximum of 4 credits. Unless otherwise specified, mathematically correct alternative solutions should be awarded appropriate credit.

(37) **[4]** Cylinder or Carol's, and an appropriate justification is given, and 14.9, and appropriate work is shown.

(38) **[4]** 4, and appropriate algebraic work is shown.

(39) **[4]** 358,800 and 1,000,000, and six-digit or numeric password, and appropriate work is shown, and an appropriate explanation is written.

Map to Core Curriculum

Content Strands	Item Numbers
Number Sense and Operations	36, 39
Algebra	3, 4, 8, 10, 11, 13, 14, 15, 16, 17, 19, 20, 22, 23, 24, 25, 26, 27, 29, 31, 35, 38
Geometry	9, 12, 21, 34, 37
Measurement	1, 28, 33
Statistics and Probability	2, 5, 6, 7, 18, 30, 32

June 12, 2013 — 1:15 to 4:15 a.m.

Part I

Allow a total of 60 credits, 2 credits for each of the following.

(1) . . . . . 1 . . . . .   (2) . . . . . 1 . . . . .   (3) . . . . . 3 . . . . .

(4) . . . . . 3 . . . . .   (5) . . . . . 4 . . . . .   (6) . . . . . 3 . . . . .

(7) . . . . . 1 . . . . .   (8) . . . . . 1 . . . . .   (9) . . . . . 3 . . . . .

(10) . . . . . 1 . . . . .   (11) . . . . . 2 . . . . .   (12) . . . . . 2 . . . . .

(13) . . . . . 3 . . . . .   (14) . . . . . 2 . . . . .   (15) . . . . . 1 . . . . .

(16) . . . . . 1 . . . . .   (17) . . . . . 2 . . . . .   (18) . . . . . 3 . . . . .

(19) . . . . . 4 . . . . .   (20) . . . . . 4 . . . . .   (21) . . . . . 4 . . . . .

(22) . . . . . 1 . . . . .   (23) . . . . . 3 . . . . .   (24) . . . . . 3 . . . . .

(25) . . . . . 4 . . . . .   (26) . . . . . 2 . . . . .   (27) . . . . . 2 . . . . .

(28) . . . . . 3 . . . . .   (29) . . . . . 3 . . . . .   (30) . . . . . 1 . . . . .

216

Part II
For each question, use the specific criteria to award a maximum of 2 credits. Unless otherwise specified, mathematically correct alternative solutions should be awarded appropriate credit.

(31) **[2]** $x > 4$, and appropriate algebraic work is shown.

(32) **[2]** 1014π, and appropriate work is shown.

(33) **[2]** 183, and appropriate work is shown.

Part III
For each question, use the specific criteria to award a maximum of 3 credits. Unless otherwise specified, mathematically correct alternative solutions should be awarded appropriate credit.

(34) **[3]** 225, 45, and 30, and appropriate work is shown.

(35) **[3]** 19, and appropriate work is shown.

(36) **[3]** $11 + \sqrt{3}$ and appropriate work is shown.

Part IV

For each question, use the specific criteria to award a maximum of 4 credits. Unless otherwise specified, mathematically correct alternative solutions should be awarded appropriate credit.

(37) **[4]** 2, and appropriate algebraic work is shown.

(38) **[4]** $\dfrac{15}{56}$, $\dfrac{20}{56}$ and $\dfrac{26}{56}$ or equivalent answers, and appropriate work is shown.

(39) **[4]** 65.86, an appropriate work is shown.

Map to Core Curriculum

Content Strands	Item Numbers
Number Sense and Operations	9, 28, 34, 36
Algebra	1, 4, 7, 10, 11, 12, 15, 16, 17, 19, 21, 22, 24, 25, 26, 27, 29, 31, 35, 37
Geometry	6, 18, 20, 30, 32, 39
Measurement	5, 23, 33
Statistics and Probability	2, 3, 8, 13, 14, 38

August 13, 2013 — 8:30 to 11:30 a.m.

Part I
Allow a total of 60 credits, 2 credits for each of the
following. Allow credit if the student
has written the correct answer instead of the numeral 1, 2, 3,
or 4.

(1) 1	(2) 1	(3) . . . . . 4 . . . .
(4) 3	(5) 2	(6) . . . . . 4 . . . .
(7) 1	(8) 3	(9) . . . . . 1 . . . .
(10) 2	(11) 2	(12) . . . . 4 . . . . .
(13) 3	(14) 2	(15) . . . 1 . . . . .
(16) 4	(17) 3	(18) . . . . 2 . . . . .
(19) 1	(20) 4	(21) . . . . 4 . . . . .
(22) 4	(23) 3	(24) . . . . 3 . . . . .
(25) 2	(26) 1	(27) . . . 2 . . . . .
(28) 3	(29) 1	(30) . . . . 2 . . . . .

Part II
For each question, use the specific criteria to award a maximum of 2 credits. Unless otherwise specified, mathematically correct alternative solutions should be awarded appropriate credit.

(31) **[2]** 475.2, and correct work is shown.

(32) **[2]** $12\sqrt{3}$, and correct work is shown.

(33) **[2]** 2295, and correct work is shown.

Part III
For each question, use the specific criteria to award a maximum of 3 credits. Unless otherwise specified, mathematically correct alternative solutions should be awarded appropriate credit.

(34) **[3]** 75.05, and correct work is shown.

(35) **[3]** 36 and 64, and correct algebraic work is shown.

(36) **[3]** 0.043, and correct work is shown.

Part IV

For each question, use the specific criteria to award a maximum of 4 credits. Unless otherwise specified, mathematically correct alternative solutions should be awarded appropriate credit.

(37) **[4]** Both equations are graphed correctly, and $(2, -5)$ and $(-2, 3)$ or $x = 2$, $y = -5$ and $x = -2$, $y = 3$ are stated.

(38) **[4]** $\dfrac{3x}{x+3}$, and correct work is shown.

(39) **[4]** P (not the same color) $= \dfrac{192}{380}$ or an equivalent answer and P (at least one red) $= \dfrac{324}{380}$ or an equivalent answer, and correct work is shown.

Map to Core Curriculum

Content Strands	Item Numbers
Number Sense and Operations	19, 32, 34
Algebra	2, 4, 5, 6, 7, 9, 10, 11, 15, 16, 17, 18, 20, 21, 23, 28, 29, 30 33, 35, 38
Geometry	8, 14, 22, 25, 26, 37
Measurement	31, 36
Statistics and Probability	1, 3, 12, 13, 24, 27, 39

NOTES:

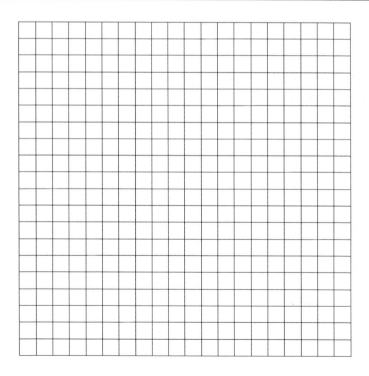

NOTES:

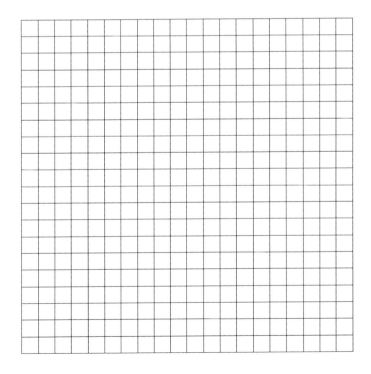

NOTES:

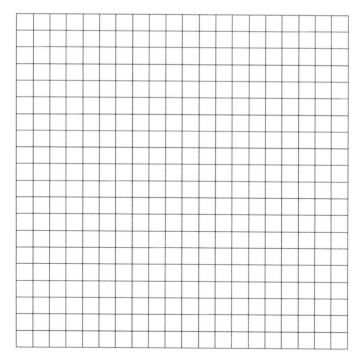

NOTES:

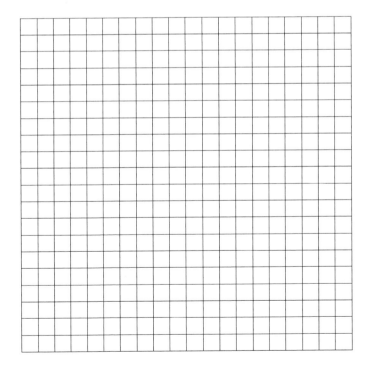

NOTES:

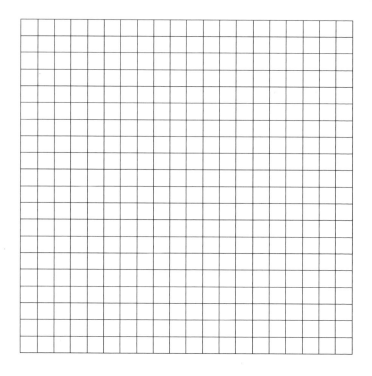